SOCIAL ISSUES, JUSTICE AND STATUS

MEANS-TESTED PROGRAMS AND TAX CREDITS FOR LOW INCOME PEOPLE

SPENDING TRENDS

SOCIAL ISSUES, JUSTICE AND STATUS

Additional books in this series can be found on Nova's website under the Series tab.

Additional E-books in this series can be found on Nova's website under the E-book tab.

ECONOMIC ISSUES, PROBLEMS AND PERSPECTIVES

Additional books in this series can be found on Nova's website under the Series tab.

Additional E-books in this series can be found on Nova's website under the E-book tab.

SOCIAL ISSUES, JUSTICE AND STATUS

MEANS-TESTED PROGRAMS AND TAX CREDITS FOR LOW INCOME PEOPLE

SPENDING TRENDS

EFRAIN B. WHITE
AND
CONNIE C. MITCHELL
EDITORS

NOVINKA

New York

For permission to use material from this book please contact us:
Telephone 631-231-7269; Fax 631-231-8175
Web Site: http://www.novapublishers.com

Library of Congress Cataloging-in-Publication Data

ISBN: 978-1-62618-552-4

Published by Nova Science Publishers, Inc. † New York

CONTENTS

PREFACE

The federal government devotes roughly one-sixth of its spending to 10 major means-tested programs and tax credits, which provide cash payments or assistance in obtaining health care, food, housing, or education to people with relatively low income or few assets. Total federal spending on these 10 programs rose more than tenfold, or by an average of about 6 percent a year, in the four decades since 1972. In this book, the Congressional Budget Office(CBO) examines the federal government's major means-tested programs and tax credits, with a focus on the factors that have affected spending on those means-tested programs. Also discussed is the projected path of spending for most of these programs over the coming decade if current laws remain in place.

Chapter 1 - The federal government devotes roughly one-sixth of its spending to 10 major means-tested programs and tax credits, which provide cash payments or assistance in obtaining health care, food, housing, or education to people with relatively low income or few assets. Those programs and credits consist of the following:

- Medicaid,
- The low-income subsidy (LIS) for Part D of Medicare (the part of Medicare that provides prescription drug benefits),
- The refundable portion of the earned income tax credit (EITC),
- The refundable portion of the child tax credit (CTC),
- Supplemental Security Income (SSI),
- Temporary Assistance for Needy Families (TANF),
- The Supplemental Nutrition Assistance Program (SNAP, formerly called the Food Stamp program),
- Child nutrition programs,

- Housing assistance programs, and
- The Federal Pell Grant Program.

In 2012, federal spending on those programs and tax credits totaled $588 billion. (Certain larger federal benefit programs, such as Social Security and Medicare, are not considered means-tested programs because they are not limited to people with specific amounts of income or assets.)

Total federal spending on those 10 programs (adjusted to exclude the effects of inflation) rose more than tenfold— or by an average of about 6 percent a year—in the four decades since 1972 (when only half of the programs existed). As a share of the economy, federal spending on those programs grew from 1 percent to almost 4 percent of gross domestic product (GDP) over that period.

Medicaid accounted for more than 40 percent of the federal spending on those programs in 2012, followed in size by SNAP. A decade from now, Medicaid will account for an even larger share of spending on those programs, the Congressional Budget Office (CBO) projects. A new means-tested program—federal subsidies to help low- and moderate-income people buy health insurance through insurance exchanges, which will begin in 2014—will be the second-largest means-tested program in 2023, CBO estimates.

Chapter 2 - This report examines the spending trends of 10 major need-tested benefit programs or groups of programs: (1) health care from Medicaid and the Children's Health Insurance Program (CHIP); (2) the refundable portion of the health insurance tax credit enacted in the 2010 health care reform law; (3) the Supplemental Nutrition Assistance Program (SNAP); (4) assisted housing; (5) financial assistance for post-secondary students (Pell Grants); (6) compensatory education grants to school districts; (7) the Earned Income Tax Credit (EITC); (8) the Additional Child Tax Credit (ACTC); (9) Supplemental Security Income (SSI); and (10) Family Support Payments. The common feature of need-tested programs is that they provide benefits, services, or funding based on a measure of limited financial resources (income and sometimes assets). However, other than that common feature, the programs differ considerably in their target populations, services, and focus.

In: Means-Tested Programs … ISBN: 978-1-62618-552-4
Editors: E. B. White and C. C. Mitchell

Chapter 1

GROWTH IN MEANS-TESTED PROGRAMS AND TAX CREDITS FOR LOW-INCOME HOUSEHOLDS*

William Carrington, Molly Dahl and Justin Falk

SUMMARY

The federal government devotes roughly one-sixth of its spending to 10 major means-tested programs and tax credits, which provide cash payments or assistance in obtaining health care, food, housing, or education to people with relatively low income or few assets. Those programs and credits consist of the following:

- Medicaid,
- The low-income subsidy (LIS) for Part D of Medicare (the part of Medicare that provides prescription drug benefits),
- The refundable portion of the earned income tax credit (EITC),
- The refundable portion of the child tax credit (CTC),
- Supplemental Security Income (SSI),
- Temporary Assistance for Needy Families (TANF),

* This is an edited, reformatted and augmented version of the Congressional Budget Office, dated February 2013.

- The Supplemental Nutrition Assistance Program (SNAP, formerly called the Food Stamp program),
- Child nutrition programs,
- Housing assistance programs, and
- The Federal Pell Grant Program.

In 2012, federal spending on those programs and tax credits totaled $588 billion. (Certain larger federal benefit programs, such as Social Security and Medicare, are not considered means-tested programs because they are not limited to people with specific amounts of income or assets.)

Total federal spending on those 10 programs (adjusted to exclude the effects of inflation) rose more than tenfold— or by an average of about 6 percent a year—in the four decades since 1972 (when only half of the programs existed).[1] As a share of the economy, federal spending on those programs grew from 1 percent to almost 4 percent of gross domestic product (GDP) over that period (see Figure 1).

Medicaid accounted for more than 40 percent of the federal spending on those programs in 2012, followed in size by SNAP. A decade from now, Medicaid will account for an even larger share of spending on those programs, the Congressional Budget Office (CBO) projects. A new means-tested program—federal subsidies to help low- and moderate-income people buy health insurance through insurance exchanges, which will begin in 2014—will be the second-largest means-tested program in 2023, CBO estimates.

What Caused Total Spending on Means-Tested Programs and Tax Credits to Rise over the Past 40 Years?

Two broad factors were responsible for the growth of spending on means-tested programs and tax credits between 1972 and 2011: increases in the number of people participating in those programs and increases in spending per participant. (This discussion focuses on the 40-year period ending in 2011 because that is the most recent year for which data on the number of participants are available for those programs.) Both of those increases were themselves the result of multiple factors. For example, the rise in participation stemmed from three important causes:

- Population growth (the U.S. population increased by almost 50 percent during that period),

- Changes in economic conditions (particularly the recession that occurred from 2007 to 2009 and the weak recovery that followed it), and
- Actions by lawmakers to create new means-tested programs and tax credits and to expand eligibility for some existing ones.

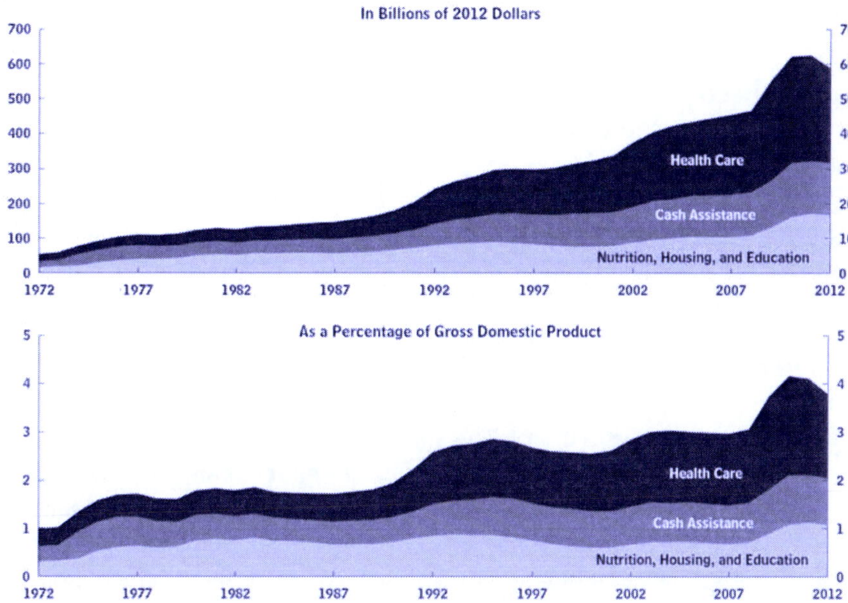

Source: Congressional Budget Office.

Notes: The health care category consists of Medicaid and the low-income subsidy for Part D of Medicare. The cash assistance category consists of the refundable portions of the earned income tax credit and the child tax credit; Supplemental Security Income; and Temporary Assistance for Needy Families (as well as its predecessor, Aid to Families with Dependent Children). The nutrition, housing, and education category comprises the Supplemental Nutrition Assistance Program; child nutrition programs; a collection of housing programs, including Section 8 housing vouchers, public housing, and several smaller programs; and the Federal Pell Grant Program. Smaller means-tested programs that provide benefits similar to those of the programs in these categories are excluded because of their size.

The data used for this figure are described in Appendix A.

Figure 1. Federal Spending on Various Categories of Means-Tested Programs and Tax Credits, 1972 to 2012.

Increases in spending per participant resulted mainly from two factors:

- Growth in the cost of providing assistance (such as rising costs for medical care), and
- Actions by lawmakers to provide more generous benefits (such as increases in SNAP benefits).

What Caused the Growth of Specific Categories of Means-Tested Programs and Tax Credits?

Roughly half of the total growth in spending between 1972 and 2011 on the means-tested programs and tax credits examined in this report came from increases in spending for health care programs—Medicaid and, to a far lesser extent, subsidies to help low-income people pay for prescription drugs under Part D of Medicare. Spending for such programs grew about 15-fold over the 1972–2011 period: from $20 billion to $305 billion. (Those and other dollar amounts for program spending in this report are presented in 2012 dollars to remove the effects of inflation.) The main reason for that growth— which averaged about 7 percent a year above the rate of inflation—was increased spending per participant. Had the amount of spending per participant in Medicaid remained unchanged between 1972 and 2011, total spending on the health care programs examined here would have been about $88 billion in 2011, or less than one-third of the actual amount.

Growth in each of two other broad categories of means-tested programs and tax credits—programs that provide cash assistance and programs that help people obtain food, housing, or education—was about equally responsible for the other half of the total increase in spending over the 1972–2011 period on the programs included in this study:

- Spending on cash assistance programs and tax credits (the largest of which is the refundable portion of the EITC) rose from $18 billion in 1972 to $151 billion in 2011—that is, by nearly 6 percent a year above the rate of inflation.
- Spending on programs that help people afford food, housing, or education (the largest of which is SNAP) rose from $17 billion to $172 billion—that is, by about 6 percent per year above the rate of inflation.

Unlike growth in spending for health care programs (pri-marily Medicaid), which stemmed mainly from greater spending per participant, growth in spending for those other programs resulted primarily from increases in the number of participants.

How Much Will Means-Tested Programs and Tax Credits Cost over the Next Decade?

If current laws that govern the means-tested programs and tax credits examined in this report do not change, total spending on those programs will grow faster than inflation over the next decade, CBO projects. However, changes in spending will vary among programs.

Spending on means-tested health care programs is projected to more than double, from $272 billion in 2012 to $624 billion in 2023 (adjusted for inflation), an average annual increase of 8 percent above the rate of inflation. That rise reflects expected growth in the cost of providing medical care; it also reflects expanded eligibility for assistance and new types of assistance to be provided under the Affordable Care Act (ACA).[2]

The ACA will not only make more people eligible for Medicaid but also allow many low- and moderate-income people who do not qualify for Medicaid to purchase federally subsidized health care coverage. Subsidizing that non-Medicaid coverage through cost-sharing subsidies and the refund-able portion of a new premium assistance tax credit is projected to cost $109 billion (in 2012 dollars) in 2023.

In contrast to spending on health care programs, total spending on the cash assistance programs and tax credits examined here is projected to fall over the next decade— from $148 billion in 2012 to $137 billion in 2023 (adjusted for inflation). That expected decline mainly stems from changes to the earned income and child tax credits that are scheduled to occur under current law.

CBO also estimates that spending on the nutrition and education programs discussed here will decline in the next 10 years, partly because spending on SNAP is projected to drop substantially as the economy continues to recover. (Unlike the other programs included in this study, the housing assistance programs rely on annual appropriations for all of their funding. In this report, CBO has not projected the size of those appropriations, which will depend on future actions by lawmakers.)[3]

An Overview of Means-Tested Programs and Tax Credits

The federal government has many programs and tax credits that are designed specifically to help people who have relatively low income or few assets. Such means-tested programs and credits—some of which are administered jointly with the states—help the people who receive benefits obtain goods or services that they might not otherwise be able to afford. For instance, SNAP enables recipients to purchase more food, Medicaid provides people with health care coverage, and Pell grants make postsecondary education more affordable for students.

The amount of money that the federal government spends annually on each means-tested program and tax credit depends on how the program or tax provision is designed. Spending for some programs, such as Medicaid and the refundable portions of tax credits, is open-ended. For example, people may enroll in Medicaid if they meet the eligibility criteria established by their state, and as people enroll and consume health care, the federal government has a legal obligation to pay a share of those benefits (the share varies from state to state). In contrast, a set amount is appropriated for SNAP annually. The amount appropriated each year is intended to cover the cost of providing benefits to all people who apply for the program and are eligible; it includes a reserve to cover unexpected costs. But if the appropriated amount does not cover those costs, either lawmakers must provide additional funds or the Department of Agriculture must reduce benefits. Other programs, such as housing assistance, receive appropriations that are not intended to cover the cost of providing benefits to everyone who applies and is eligible. Lawmakers furnish a specific amount of money for such programs each year, and if it runs out, no further benefits are provided in that year.

In this analysis, CBO focuses on the federal government's major means-tested programs and tax credits, which it groups into three categories:

- *Health care programs*—Medicaid; the low-income subsidy for Part D of Medicare (which covers prescription drugs); and, beginning in 2014, assistance for low- and moderate-income people who purchase health insurance through the new insurance exchanges.
- *Cash assistance programs and refundable tax credits*— The refundable portions of the earned income tax credit and the child tax credit; Supplemental Security Income; and Temporary Assistance for

Needy Families (as well as its predecessor, Aid to Families with Dependent Children).

- *Nutrition, housing, and education assistance programs*— The Supplemental Nutrition Assistance Program; child nutrition programs, including the National School Lunch Program and the School Breakfast Program; a collection of housing assistance programs, including assistance authorized under section 8 of the United States Housing Act of 1937; and the Federal Pell Grant Program.

Federal spending on those means-tested programs and tax credits totaled $588 billion in 2012 (see Figure 2). That amount—roughly one-sixth of federal spending—was more than the government spent on Medicare in 2012 and less than it spent on Social Security or defense.

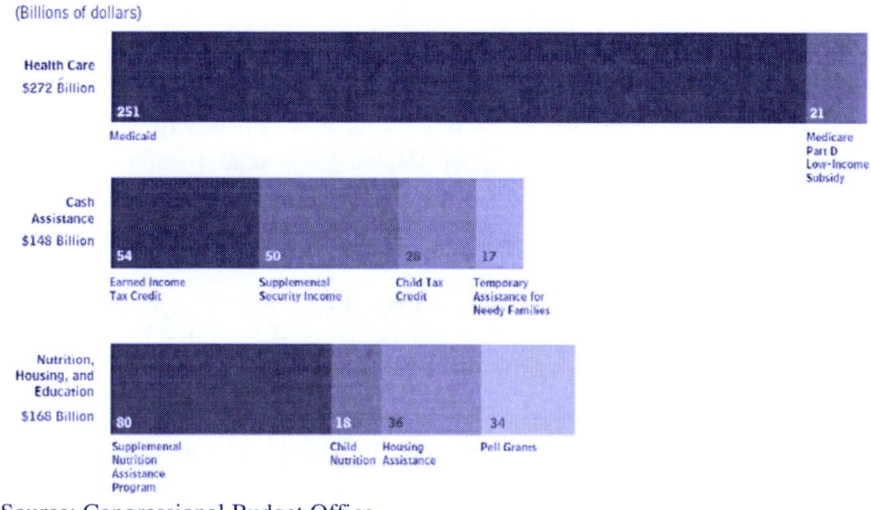

Source: Congressional Budget Office.
Note: The data used for this figure are described in Appendix A.

Figure 2. Federal Spending on Selected Means-Tested Programs and Tax Credits, 2012.

This study discusses the factors that have affected spend-ing on those means-tested programs and analyzes trends in spending for each of them over the past 40 years (the period that CBO typically looks at when comparing bud-get projections with historical spending and revenues). The study also examines the projected path of spending for most of those programs over the coming decade if current laws remain in place.

Many other federal programs and parts of the tax system that improve people's well-being are not included in this analysis. For example, social insurance and other government assistance programs that are not means-tested— such as Social Security, Medicare, and unemployment insurance—are not considered in this report. Such pro-grams are classified as means-tested only if they directly target assistance toward low-income people. Some programs instead provide assistance to groups of people among whom poverty is common, such as Native Americans or students at schools that draw heavily from low-income families. Those programs are not considered in this analysis.

This report also does not address features of the federal tax system that provide significant financial assistance for the acquisition of goods and services (such as housing and health care) but that mainly benefit people with relatively high income. Those features—which include exclusions from taxable income, itemized deductions, and preferential tax rates on capital gains and dividends— can resemble government spending programs by providing financial assistance for specific activities, entities, or groups of people. However, because they are not targeted toward low-income people, they are not included in this report.[4]

SOURCES OF PAST GROWTH IN MEANS-TESTED PROGRAMS AND TAX CREDITS

Federal spending on means-tested programs and tax credits has grown throughout the past four decades. Adjusted to remove the effects of inflation, total spending on the programs and credits included in this analysis rose from $55 billion in 1972 (when just 5 of the 10 programs existed) to $628 billion in 2011, before declining to $588 billion in 2012, largely because a temporary increase in the federal government's share of Medicaid costs expired in June 2011 (see Table 1). As spending on those programs increased, so did the amount of benefits they provided to low-income people. (For a discussion of how the benefits of means-tested programs are distributed among people with different incomes, see Box 1 on page 8.)

The growth in total spending for means-tested programs and tax credits over the past four decades resulted from an increase in the number of people participating in such programs as well as from a rise in the amount of spending per participant. This section outlines the major factors that caused those developments; the next section provides details for individual programs. (The analysis focuses on the 40-year period ending in 2011, the most recent year for which data on the number of participants are available for those programs.)

Table 1. Federal Spending on Various Categories of Means-Tested Programs and Tax Credits, Selected Years

	1972	1991	2011	2012
In Billions of 2012 Dollars				
Health Care	20	82	305	272
Cash Assistance	18	51	151	148
Nutrition, Housing, and Education	17	73	172	168
Total	**55**	**206**	**628**	**588**
As a Percentage of Gross Domestic Product				
Health Care	0.4	0.9	2.0	1.7
Cash Assistance	0.3	0.6	1.0	1.0
Nutrition, Housing, and Education	0.3	0.8	1.1	1.1
Total	**1.0**	**2.2**	**4.1**	**3.8**

Source: Congressional Budget Office.

Notes: The health care category consists of Medicaid and the low-income subsidy for Part D of Medicare. The cash assistance category consists of the refundable portions of the earned income tax credit and the child tax credit; Supplemental Security Income; and Temporary Assistance for Needy Families (as well as its predecessor, Aid to Families with Dependent Children). The nutrition, housing, and education category comprises the Supplemental Nutrition Assistance Program; child nutrition programs; a collection of housing programs, including Section 8 housing vouchers, public housing, and several smaller programs; and the Federal Pell Grant Program. Smaller means-tested programs that provide benefits similar to those of the programs in these categories are excluded because of their size.

The data shown here are described in Appendix A.

Increased Participation

For most of the programs and tax credits, the number of people receiving benefits grew substantially between 1972 and 2011 because of such factors as population growth, economic downturns, or policy changes that expanded the programs and credits or added new ones. (Calculating the total number of participants in all programs is difficult, however. Participation is measured differently in different programs, as explained in Appendix B, and a person can receive benefits from multiple means-tested programs at the same time.)

Changes in the Size of the Population

The number of people living in the United States rose by 49 percent during the 1972–2011 period, from 210 million to 312 million. As the population grew, so did the number of people participating in means-tested programs. However, participation in the programs and tax credits examined here tended to increase much faster than the population did. For instance, participation in Medicaid and SNAP more than tripled between 1972 and 2011 (to 53 million and 45 million, respectively, from 17 million and 11 million).

Changes in Economic Conditions

Many means-tested programs are open to anyone who meets the eligibility criteria; thus, if economic conditions worsen and income declines, the number of people taking part in those programs tends to increase. For example, in 2007, the unemployment rate was 4.6 percent, and roughly 37 million people lived in families with income below the Census Bureau's federal poverty thresholds.

By 2010, the unemployment rate had more than doubled, to 9.6 percent, and the number of people in families with income below the poverty thresholds had risen to about 46 million. (The figures for families include single adults.) Participation in SNAP and Medicaid grew substantially during those years and has remained relatively high since then.

Policy Changes That Created or Expanded Programs and Tax Credits

Between 1972 and 2011, lawmakers created several new means-tested programs and tax credits and extended the benefits of some existing programs to people who were previously ineligible. Five of the 10 programs and tax credits examined here were established after 1972: Pell grants, SSI, and the EITC were all instituted in the mid-1970s; payments for the child tax credit were first made in 1999; and the Medicare Part D LIS program began paying benefits in 2006.

Those five programs accounted for about 30 percent of the spending in 2011 for the programs discussed in this report. In some cases, such as with SSI, those new programs replaced federal or state programs that had served a similar purpose. In total, however, the new programs increased the number of people who participated in any means-tested program.

Expansions of eligibility also boosted participation in existing programs by extending benefits to people who had not qualified for them before. For example, a series of laws enacted in the 1980s and 1990s widened eligibility for Medicaid. In addition, lawmakers have periodically expanded eligibility for some of the programs and credits created after 1972, such as the EITC.

Increased Spending per Participant

In addition to an upsurge in participation, the average amount spent for each participant grew substantially for a number of programs and tax credits over the 1972–2011 period. That increase was primarily attributable to the rising cost of providing services and to changes in the size of benefits provided. (Like total participation in means-tested programs, total spending per participant is difficult to calculate because of differences among programs in how participation is measured; see Appendix B.)

Changes in the Cost of Providing Services

For some pro-grams, spending per participant (adjusted for inflation) rose because the cost of providing services grew more quickly than inflation. The most significant example of that phenomenon was increases in the cost of medical care (relative to the costs of other goods and services), which played a major part in raising the average cost of Medicaid per participant. Similarly, increases in the price of food (relative to the prices of other goods and services), though less dramatic than increases in the cost of medical care, boosted per-person spending for SNAP in the past decade.

Policy Changes That Increased Benefits

Actions by lawmakers, such as raising the maximum benefit that people can receive, also increased spending per participant for some programs and tax credits. For instance, lawmakers raised the maximum amounts available through the EITC several times over the past 25 years and doubled the maximum amounts available through the child tax credit in the Economic Growth and Tax Relief Reconciliation Act of 2001 (EGTRRA).

More recently, the American Recovery and Reinvestment Act of 2009 (ARRA) increased the benefits available through those credits, raised the maximum SNAP benefit, and boosted the federal share of Medicaid costs, all on a temporary basis.

PAST GROWTH IN SPECIFIC PROGRAMS AND TAX CREDITS

Of the $628 billion (in 2012 dollars) that the federal government spent in 2011 on the means-tested programs and tax credits considered here, health care programs accounted for $305 billion (most of it spent on Medic-aid); cash assistance programs and tax credits accounted for $151 billion; and programs that help people obtain food, housing, and education accounted for $172 billion (see Table 1). The sources of growth described above have played different roles in determining the path of spending for those different categories of means-tested programs over the years—and in some cases for different programs within a category. Increases in spending per participant were the main reason for the growth of spending on Medicaid, whereas increases in participation were generally the largest factor behind the overall growth of spending on cash assistance programs and tax credits and on nutrition, housing, and education programs.[5] (The data used for this analysis, which come from various sources and differ in many ways, are described in Appendix A.)

Means-Tested Health Care Programs

The government provides health insurance coverage to low-income people through Medicaid. It also provides prescription drug benefits to low-income beneficiaries of the Medicare program through the low-income subsidy in Part D of Medicare. Total spending on those means-tested programs increased from $20 billion (0.4 percent of GDP) in 1972 to $305 billion (2.0 percent of GDP) in 2011, adjusted for inflation. Medicaid accounted for most of that spending (see Table 2 and Figure 3).[6]

Medicaid

Medicaid provides health insurance coverage to eligible low-income people, including children, pregnant women, parents of dependent children, elderly people, and people with disabilities. The program, which was established pursuant to title XIX of the Social Security Amendments of 1965, is financed jointly by the federal government and state governments. States administer the program within broad federal parameters, and the federal government reimburses states for some of their Medicaid costs at specific matching rates.

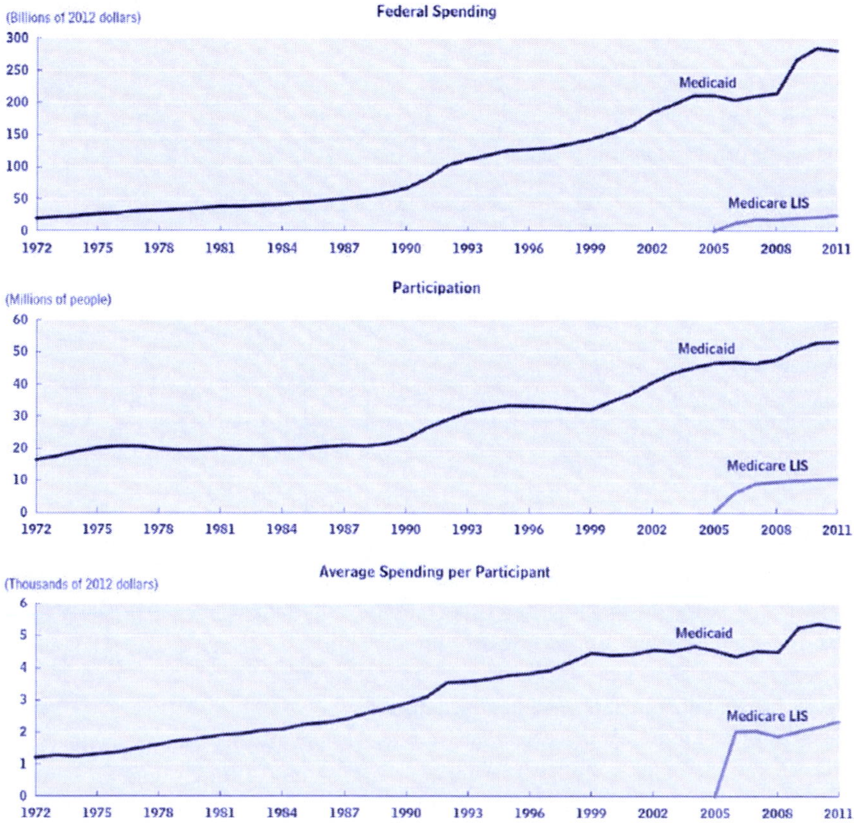

Source: Congressional Budget Office.
Notes: The data used for this figure are described in Appendix A.
Medicare LIS = low-income subsidy for Part D of Medicare.

Figure 3. Growth in Selected Means-Tested Programs That Provide Health Care, 1972 to 2011.

In 2011, about half of Medicaid's enrollees were children in low-income families, and another one-quarter were either the parents of those children or low-income pregnant women. People who were elderly or disabled constituted the remaining one-quarter of enrollees. Expenses tend to be higher for beneficiaries who are elderly or disabled, many of whom require long-term care, than for other beneficiaries.

Table 2. Federal Spending on and Participation in Selected Means-Tested Programs That Provide Health Care, Selected Years

	1972	1991	2011
	Medicaid		
Federal Spending			
Billions of 2012 dollars	20	82	280
Percentage of gross domestic product	0.4	0.9	1.8
Participation			
Millions of people	16.5	26.3	53.2
Percentage of U.S. residents	7.9	10.4	17.0
Average Spending per Participant (2012 dollars)[a]	1,200	3,100	5,300
	Medicare Part D Low-Income Subsidy		
Federal Spending			
Billions of 2012 dollars	0	0	25
Percentage of gross domestic product	0	0	0.2
Participation			
Millions of people	0	0	10.6
Percentage of U.S. residents	0	0	3.4
Average Spending per Participant (2012 dollars)	0	0	2,300

Source: Congressional Budget Office.

Notes: Benefits under the low-income subsidy for Part D of Medicare were first paid in 2006.

The data shown here are described in Appendix A.

[a.] The cost of benefits differs substantially among groups of Medicaid participants. In 2010, for example, average spending per enrollee was $10,200 for people under age 65 with disabilities, $9,500 for people age 65 or older, $2,400 for nondisabled adults under age 65, and $1,800 for nondisabled children.

About 30 percent of federal Medicaid spending is for long-term care, which includes nursing home services, home health care, and certain other medical and social services for people with long-term health needs.

In 2011, Medicaid accounted for almost half of total spending on long-term care services and almost two-fifths of total spending on nursing home care in the United States. Overall, people who were elderly or disabled accounted for about two-thirds of Medicaid spending.[7]

BOX 1. THE DISTRIBUTION OF FEDERAL SPENDING ON MEANS-TESTED PROGRAMS AND TAX CREDITS BY HOUSEHOLD INCOME

Federal spending on the means-tested programs and tax credits examined in this study provides various types of support to households. To examine how that support differs among households at different income levels, the Congressional Budget Office estimated how the federal government's total spending on those programs in 2006—about $440 billion (in 2012 dollars)—was allocated among households in five income groups (or quintiles), ranked according to an annual measure of market income.[1] (The distributional analysis focuses on 2006 because, when the analysis began, that was the most recent year for which necessary data were available from the Internal Revenue Service's Statistics of Income Division.)

On average, the federal government gave decreasing amounts of means-tested support to households higher up on the income scale. That support averaged $8,800 for households in the lowest income quintile, $4,000 for those in the next-to-lowest quintile, and $1,600 for households in the middle quintile (see the table at right).[2] The largest source of means-tested spending per household for each of the income groups was Medicaid.

Not only was the amount of federal means-tested support largest for the lowest-income households, but that spending amounted to the greatest share of market income for such households. Federal spending on means-tested programs and tax credits boosted average income by 92 percent for households in the lowest income quintile and by 3 percent for households in the middle quintile.

For most of the programs examined in this report, average spending per household tended to decline as income increased—partly because fewer people in the higher income quintiles were eligible for benefits, and partly because among those eligible, benefits tended to be lower for people with higher income.[3] For the earned income and child tax credits, however, combined spending on the refundable portions of the two credits was largest for households with income in the next-to-lowest quintile. Households without income are ineligible for those credits, and the amount of the earned income tax credit initially increases with earnings and then remains steady at the maximum benefit before starting to decline as earnings grow further.

Average Federal Spending per Household on Selected Means-Tested Programs and Tax Credits, by Income Group, 2006

(2012 dollars)					
	Lowest Quintile	**Second Quintile**	**Third Quintile**	**Fourth Quintile**	**Highest Quintile**
Health Care					
Medicaid[a]	3,300	1,500	700	400	300
Medicare Part D low-income subsidy	400	100	100	*	*
Cash Assistance					
Earned income and child tax credits[b]	800	1,100	400	200	100
Supplemental Security Income	1,100	300	200	100	100
TANF	500	200	*	*	*
Nutrition, Housing, and Education					
SNAP	1,200	300	*	*	*
Child nutrition	200	200	100	*	*
Housing assistance	1,100	100	*	*	*
Pell grants	200	300	100	100	*
Total					
In 2012 dollars	**8,800**	**4,000**	**1,600**	**800**	**500**
As a percentage of market income	**92**	**11**	**3**	**1**	**
Memorandum:					
Average Market Income	9,600	35,500	61,600	96,400	271,000

Source: Congressional Budget Office based on data from the Internal Revenue Service and the Census Bureau.

Notes: Income groups are defined by ranking all people according to their market income, adjusted for household size, and dividing that ranking into fifths (quintiles). Market income includes income from work, business income, capital gains and other capital income, and income received in retirement for past services. A household consists of the people who share a housing unit, regardless of their relationships. Each quintile contains equal numbers of people, except the lowest quintile; households with negative income (business or investment losses larger than other income) are not included.

The numbers shown here represent average federal spending on a program for all households in a given income quintile, not just households that participate in the program.

TANF = Temporary Assistance for Needy Families; SNAP = Supplemental Nutrition Assistance Program; * = between zero and $50; ** = between zero and 0.5 percent.

a. Does not include Medicaid spending for beneficiaries residing in long-term care institutions and other Medicaid spending that cannot be allocated to specific households.

b. Includes only the portions of the earned income tax credit and the child tax credit that are paid to tax filers because they exceed filers' tax liabilities.

1. Market income includes income from work, business income, capital gains and other capital income, and income received in retirement for past services.
2. The table presents average income and spending amounts for the five income groups. Within each group, income and benefits received vary considerably, but this analysis does not examine that variation.
3. High-income households are shown as receiving means-tested assistance for several reasons. Some households have income that varies over the course of a year, and they may qualify for benefits when their monthly income is low, even though their annual income is high. In addition, some people who qualify for benefits on the basis of their own low income live in high-income households. Also, the data include some misreporting of income, program participation, and benefit amounts.

Federal spending on Medicaid has grown substantially since the early years of the program, the result of rising per-person health care costs and interactions between policy decisions made at the federal and state levels. Between 1972 and 2011, federal spending on the pro-gram grew from $20 billion (0.4 percent of GDP) to $280 billion (1.8 percent of GDP), an average increase of 7 percent per year above the rate of inflation. Federal spending climbed especially sharply in recent years because of a temporary increase in federal matching rates authorized by ARRA (which was phased out in June 2011) and because of large increases in participation resulting from the recent recession.

Both the amount of money spent on each Medicaid participant and the total number of participants swelled over the past four decades:

- Federal spending per participant more than quadrupled, from $1,200 in 1972 to $5,300 in 2011 (in 2012 dollars), accounting for the majority of the total increase in Medicaid spending during that period.
- The number of people enrolled in Medicaid more than tripled, from 17 million in 1972 to 53 million in 2011.

Many factors were responsible for those increases. Some—such as general growth in health care costs, shifts in the composition of Medicaid beneficiaries, changes in the services covered by the program, and the availability of supplemental payments to health care providers—mainly affected spending per person. Other factors—such as population growth and policy changes at the state and federal levels that increased eligibility for Medicaid—boosted the number of program participants.

Average Spending per Participant. Health care costs per person have risen throughout the economy at a rate that has outstripped the pace of economic growth, in part because of the emergence, adoption, and widespread diffusion of new medical technologies and services. Although the growth of per capita health care costs varies among different forms of health insurance and over different time periods, increases in Medicaid spending per participant partly reflect growth in health care costs in general.

Changes in the composition of Medicaid beneficiaries have also affected the growth of program spending over time. In some cases, those changes have reduced spending per participant, and in other cases they have increased it. For example, the share of Medicaid beneficiaries who have disabilities—the most costly type of beneficiary, on average—rose from 12 percent in 1975 to 17 percent in 2008. At the same time, the share of beneficiaries who are children—the least costly type of beneficiary—also rose, from 48 percent in 1975 to 51 percent in 2008. (Data on the composition of Medicaid beneficiaries are not available for the full 1972–2011 period.)

In addition, policy changes have expanded the services that Medicaid covers. Over the years, modifications to federal law have required states to cover more services and have allowed states to be reimbursed for more optional benefits. Many states have responded by adding benefits to their programs. States have also been permitted to offer special services, through waivers of federal program requirements, to subgroups of the eligible population. Such waivers have been used, for instance, to expand home- and community-based long-term care services for people who meet Medicaid's criteria for nursing home care. (States are allowed to cap the number of participants in such waiver programs, because more elderly and disabled people may seek those services than would have sought nursing home care.)[8]

States have also had increasing opportunities to receive federal matching funds for supplemental payments to health care providers. Most of those payments—such as ones made to hospitals that provide disproportionate shares of Medicaid services and uncompensated care, relative to other hospitals—did not exist in 1972. In 2012, such supplemental payments made up about 9 percent of Medicaid spending.

Number of Participants. The U.S. population grew by 49 percent between 1972 and 2011, which accounts for some of the more-than-threefold increase in the number of Medicaid participants during that time. More important, the share of the population receiving Medicaid benefits more than doubled over that period—from 8 percent to 17 percent—mostly because of expansions in eligibility for the program. When Medicaid began, participating states were required to cover only people (with a few exceptions) who were eligible for benefits under certain cash assistance programs, such as Aid to Families with Dependent Children, the predecessor to TANF. Beyond those groups, states could cover a limited number of optional populations that were not eligible for cash assistance, including some children from low-income families and certain people who had high medical expenses relative to their income. Over the years, federal law was modified repeatedly to expand eligibility, either automatically or at the discretion of the states. For instance, a series of laws enacted in the 1980s and early 1990s extended Medicaid coverage to additional pregnant women and children from low-income families who were ineligible for cash assistance.

In addition, states have taken advantage of opportunities to convert programs that they had previously financed entirely with their own funds into programs for which they could claim federal matching payments under Medicaid.

As one example, the federal share of Medicaid spending on mental health services and hospitals has increased substantially over the years. States that had funded most of those services themselves gradually shifted the delivery of mental health services in such a way as to become eligible for Medicaid reimbursement, enabling them to receive federal matching payments for those expenditures.[9]

Medicare Part D Low-Income Subsidy

Medicare is the federal government's health insurance program for people age 65 and older (and for younger people with certain disabilities); Part D is the portion of Medicare that covers prescription drugs. Medicare as a whole is not limited to low-income people, but the low-income subsidy offered through Part D (also known as the Extra Help program or LIS) is means-tested. It subsidizes prescription drug benefits for Medicare beneficiaries whose household income is no more than 150 percent of the federal poverty guidelines and whose assets do not exceed certain thresholds.[10] Like the rest of Part D, the low-income subsidy was authorized by the Medicare Prescription Drug, Improvement, and Modernization Act of 2003. Before that law was enacted, many low-income Medicare beneficiaries received prescription drug coverage through Medicaid.

In 2007, the first full fiscal year that the program was in operation, LIS benefits were paid to 9 million recipients at a cost of $18 billion—or an average of $2,000 per participant. Both participation and spending per participant increased gradually over the next four years. In 2011, roughly $25 billion in LIS benefits were distributed to 10.6 million people, for an average cost of $2,300 per participant.

Means-Tested Cash Assistance Programs and Tax Credits

Four of the programs and tax credits examined in this study provide cash payments to people with low income. The refundable portions of the earned income tax credit and child tax credit subsidize the earnings of workers with low earnings; Supplemental Security Income provides assistance to disabled or elderly people; and Temporary Assistance for Needy Families is a source of cash assistance to families with low income. Combined spending on those programs rose from $18 billion in 1972 to $151 billion in 2011, or from 0.3 percent to 1.0 percent of GDP, an average annual increase that was almost 6 percent above the rate of inflation (see Table 3 and Figure 4). Growth in the two tax credits over the past 20 years was responsible for the majority of that increase. (The EITC and CTC are refundable tax credits, meaning that if the amount of credit for which someone is eligible exceeds his or her tax liabilities, the taxpayer receives the excess as a payment. In this analysis, CBO's estimates of spending and participation for those tax credits apply only to such payments, which are usually called the refundable portions of the credits.)[11]

Earned Income Tax Credit

The EITC provides cash assistance through the federal income tax system to tax filers on the basis of their family size and earnings. The credit is not available to tax filers without earnings. It increases with people's earnings, up to a maximum credit amount for a given family size.

The credit remains at that maximum size as earnings rise, until, at a certain amount of earnings, the credit begins to decrease. When earnings reach specific thresholds, tax filers are no longer eligible for the EITC. In 2012, those thresholds ranged from $13,980 for a single worker without children to $50,270 for a married couple with three or more children.

Table 3. Federal Spending on and Participation in Selected Means-Tested Programs and Tax Credits That Provide Cash Assistance, Selected Years

	1972	1991	2011
	Earned Income Tax Credit[a]		
Federal Spending			
Billions of 2012 dollars	0	8	55
Percentage of gross domestic product	0	0.1	0.4
Participation			
Millions of tax filers	0	8.7	25.2
Percentage of all tax filers	0	7.6	17.7
Average Spending per Participant (2012 dollars)	0	900	2,200
	Supplemental Security Income		
Federal Spending			
Billions of 2012 dollars	0	23	49
Percentage of gross domestic product	0	0.2	0.3
Participation			
Millions of people	0	4.5	7.8
Percentage of U.S. residents	0	1.8	2.5
Average Spending per Participant (2012 dollars)	0	5,000	6,300
	Child Tax Credit[a]		
Federal Spending			
Billions of 2012 dollars	0	0	28
Percentage of gross domestic product	0	0	0.2
Participation			
Millions of tax filers	0	0	21.0
Percentage of all tax filers	0	0	14.7
Average Spending per Participant (2012 dollars)	0	0	1,300
	AFDC/TANF[b]		
Federal Spending			
Billions of 2012 dollars	18	20	18
Percentage of gross domestic product	0.3	0.2	0.1

Source: Congressional Budget Office.

Notes: The Supplemental Security Income program began paying benefits in 1974, the earned income tax credit in 1976, and the child tax credit in 1999. The data shown here are described in Appendix A. AFDC = Aid to Families with Dependent Children; TANF = Temporary Assistance for Needy Families.

a. Numbers for the tax credits consist only of amounts that are paid to tax filers because they exceed filers' tax liabilities. (In addition to those payments, the tax credits reduce federal revenues by lowering the amount that tax filers owe. For the earned income tax credit, those reductions were zero in 1972, $2 billion in 1991, and $5 billion in 2011; for the child tax credit, they were zero in 1972 and 1991 and $29 billion in 2011.).

b. Comprehensive data on participation and spending per participant are not available for TANF.

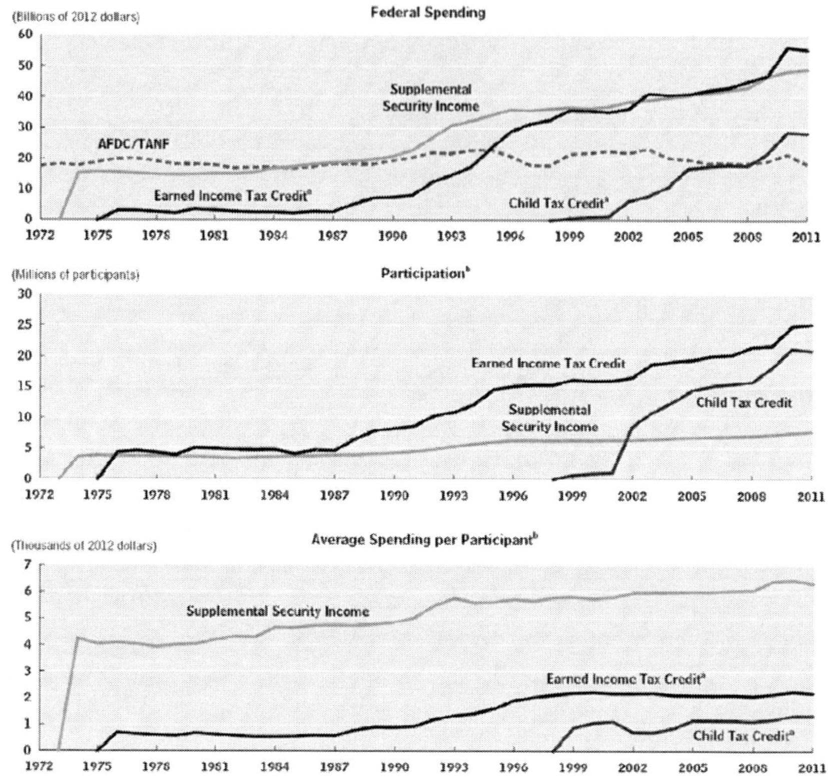

Source: Congressional Budget Office.

Notes: The data used for this figure are described in Appendix A.

AFDC = Aid to Families with Dependent Children; TANF = Temporary Assistance for Needy Families.

[a.] Numbers for the tax credits consist only of amounts that are paid to tax filers because they exceed filers' tax liabilities.

[b.] For the Supplemental Security Income program, participation is measured as the number of people who receive benefits. For the tax credits, participation is measured as the number of tax-filing units that receive refundable credits. (Such units can contain more than one person.) Comprehensive data on participation and spending per participant are not available for TANF.

Figure 4. Growth in Selected Means-Tested Programs and Tax Credits That Provide Cash Assistance, 1972 to 2011.

The first EITC payments were made in 1976. Spending on the refundable portion of the credit remained relatively small through the 1980s; in 1991, it totaled $8 billion (0.1 percent of GDP). By 2011, when nearly one-fifth of tax filers claimed the refundable EITC, that spending had risen to $55 billion (0.4 percent of GDP). The average EITC payment in that year was $2,200. (The nonrefundable portion of the EITC, which is not included in this analysis, reduced federal revenues by $5 billion in 2011.)

Most of the growth in EITC spending after 1976 stemmed from policy changes that increased the maximum credit and the range of income over which the EITC is available. The maximum credit was raised for all families with children in the 1980s and 1990s; and since 2000, lawmakers have expanded the credit for married couples filing joint tax returns (in both EGTRRA and ARRA) and for families with three or more children (in ARRA). Largely because of those changes, both the percentage of tax filers receiving EITC payments and the average amount of those payments more than tripled between 1976 and 2011. The total number of people filing tax returns also rose during that period, but that increase accounted for a relatively small portion of the growth in EITC spending.

Supplemental Security Income

SSI was established by the Social Security Amendments of 1972 and began paying benefits in 1974 to low-income people who were age 65 or older, blind, or disabled. SSI was designed to replace a wide range of earlier federally supported programs run by the states that provided cash assistance to low-income people who were elderly, blind, or disabled. The maximum monthly SSI benefit in 2012 was $698 for an individual and $1,048 for a couple. People receive the maximum benefit only if they have no more than minimal income from other specified sources. If they do have other income, such as more than $65 a month in wages or $20 in Social Security benefits, their SSI benefits are reduced.[12] In addition to low income, SSI applicants must have assets below certain thresholds to qualify for the program. In 2011, 70 percent of SSI participants were blind or disabled adults younger than 65, 16 percent were blind or disabled children, and 14 percent were people age 65 or older.

Federal spending on the SSI program has risen gradually over the years, from $16 billion in 1975 to $49 billion in 2011, an average annual increase of about 3 percent above the rate of inflation. Roughly 60 percent of that rise is attributable to increases in participation; the rest resulted from growth in spending per participant.

The number of people receiving SSI benefits doubled between 1975 and 2011, from 3.9 million to 7.8 million. About half of the increase in participation can be attributed to population growth, but the share of the population participating in the program also rose, from 1.8 percent in 1975 to 2.5 percent in 2011. In particular, the percentages of disabled children and disabled adults under age 65 who participated in SSI grew. One reason is that the 1990 Supreme Court ruling in *Sullivan v. Zebley* allowed children to qualify for SSI on the basis of functional limitations rather than specific medical diagnoses, which increased the percentage of disabled children eligible for the program.[13] The share of non-elderly adults eligible for SSI rose in part because the Social Security Disability Reform Act of 1984 loosened standards for defining disability. In addition, outreach efforts in the early 1990s to increase awareness of the pro-gram probably raised the percentage of disabled children and nonelderly disabled adults participating in SSI. By contrast, the share of people age 65 or older who were eligible for and ultimately received SSI benefits declined between 1975 and 2011, mainly because people in that age range have become more likely to have Social Security benefits that are high enough to make them ineligible for SSI. In recent years, the recession and slow recovery have lowered income and thus made more disabled people eligible to receive SSI benefits.

Spending per SSI participant rose by 57 percent between 1975 and 2011, from $4,000 to $6,300 (after adjustment for inflation). Part of the reason is that the inflation measure that CBO used for that adjustment, the personal consumption expenditures (PCE) price index, grows more slowly than the measure used to increase SSI payments each year.[14] In addition, the Omnibus Budget Reconciliation Act of 1990 specified that SSI benefits would no longer be reduced if someone received an EITC payment.

Child Tax Credit

The CTC allows families to claim a tax credit of up to $1,000 for each child under 17 years old. In 2011, the refundable portion of the credit went almost entirely to families with income below $50,000. The reason is that families with higher income typically owe enough federal income tax that the entire CTC goes to offset the amount they owe, with nothing left over to be paid to the tax filer. In 2011, spending on the refundable portion of the CTC totaled $28 billion. (The nonrefundable portion lowered people's total income tax liabilities—and thus federal revenues—by $29 billion in 2011, but only 30 percent of that went to tax filers with income below $50,000.) Like the EITC, the refundable portion of the child tax credit is not available to families without earnings.

The CTC was created by the Taxpayer Relief Act of 1997 and has been expanded several times since then. Initially, the refundable portion of the credit was available only to families with three or more children and only as an offset to their share of payroll taxes that had not been offset by the EITC. The CTC provided a maximum benefit of $400 per child (rising to $500 in 1999). A series of legislative changes, beginning with EGTRRA in 2001, extended the refundable portion of the credit to families with one or two children and raised the maximum benefit to $1,000 per child. As a result, spending on the refundable part of the CTC increased from $1 billion in 2001 to $28 billion in 2011, as the share of tax filers receiving a payment because of the credit grew from 1 percent to 15 percent.

The average CTC payment hovered around $1,000 from 2001 to 2011. That stability was the result of two countervailing trends. On the one hand, the tax filers who became newly eligible for the CTC during that period had fewer than three children and thus received smaller credits, on average. On the other hand, the expanded refundability of the credit and the increase in the maximum benefit per child substantially boosted the average amount spent on filers with three or more children.

Temporary Assistance for Needy Families

TANF provides cash and other forms of assistance to some families with little or no income. It was created by the Personal Responsibility and Work Opportunity Reconciliation Act of 1996 (PRWORA) as a successor to the Aid to Families with Dependent Children program (AFDC), which began in 1935. Like AFDC, TANF makes monthly cash payments to low-income families at a level determined by state-specific formulas and is administered by state agencies. TANF differs from its predecessor in various ways, however. In particular, whereas AFDC allowed families to receive assistance for as long as they were otherwise eligible, TANF imposes a five-year lifetime limit on benefits. In addition, TANF has a much greater emphasis than AFDC did on encouraging recipients to work. Reflecting that emphasis, less than 50 percent of TANF spending goes to cash assistance. The rest pays for various services for low-income families with children, including child care, transportation to work, and other types of work-related assistance. (Some participants in TANF receive work-support services but not cash payments.)

Between 1972 and 1996, spending on the AFDC pro-gram rose from $18 billion to $21 billion (in 2012 dollars).[15] That growth was slower than the growth of the economy; consequently, AFDC spending declined from 0.3 percent of GDP to 0.2 percent over that period. Under PRWORA, states had to transition from AFDC to TANF by July 1997. Since 1998, the primary source of federal funding for TANF has been state family assistance grants, which have amounted to about $16 billion a year. Inflation-adjusted spending on TANF has been fairly stable since the late 1990s. By 2011, it equaled 0.1 percent of GDP.[16]

As a rising share of spending went toward work support and other services, the number of people receiving cash assistance through TANF declined. When the AFDC program ended, 13 million people were recipients of cash assistance; in 2011, TANF provided cash payments to about 4 million people. (Data on the number of people receiving other forms of assistance from TANF are not available.)

Means-Tested Nutrition, Housing, and Education Programs

The other programs included in this analysis help people obtain food, housing, and education. They consist of SNAP, child nutrition programs (such as the National School Lunch Program and the School Breakfast Program), various programs that subsidize the cost of housing for low-income people, and the Federal Pell Grant Program. Combined spending on those programs rose from $17 billion (0.3 percent of GDP) in 1972 to $172 billion (1.1 percent of GDP) in 2011 (see Table 4)—an average annual increase of about 6 percent above the rate of inflation. Approximately 40 percent of that increase came from growth in spending on SNAP and Pell grants since 2007 (see Figure 5).

Supplemental Nutrition Assistance Program

SNAP, formerly called the Food Stamp program, provides benefits to households with low income to help them purchase food.[17] Versions of the program have been in place since 1939. People now receive SNAP benefits through an electronic benefit transfer card that they use to buy approved food at participating stores. In 2010, about three out of four households that received SNAP benefits included a child, someone age 60 or older, or a disabled person. SNAP recipients generally live in households with very low income—an average of about $9,000 in 2010.

Over the 1972–2011 period, spending on SNAP increased from $9 billion (0.2 percent of GDP) to $79 billion (0.5 percent of GDP). A rising participation rate and higher spending per participant were the major reasons—accounting for 44 percent and 37 percent of that increase, respectively. Population growth accounted for the other 19 percent of the increase in spending over that period.

Table 4. Federal Spending on and Participation in Selected Means-Tested Programs That Assist with Nutrition, Housing, and Education, Selected Years

	1972	1991	2011
		SNAP	
Federal Spending			
Billions of 2012 dollars	9	31	79
Percentage of gross domestic product	0.2	0.3	0.5
Participation			
Millions of people	11.1	22.6	44.7
Percentage of U.S. residents	5.3	8.9	14.3
Average Spending per Participant (2012 dollars)	800	1,300	1,800
		Child Nutrition[a]	
Federal Spending			
Billions of 2012 dollars	3	9	18
Percentage of gross domestic product	0.1	0.1	0.1
		Housing Assistance	
Federal Spending			
Billions of 2012 dollars	5	26	39
Percentage of gross domestic product	0.1	0.3	0.3
Participation			
Millions of households	1.5	4.4	4.8
Percentage of all households	2.1	4.1	3.7
Average Spending per Participant (2012 dollars)	3,300	5,800	8,000
		Pell Grants	
Federal Spending			
Billions of 2012 dollars	0	8	36
Percentage of gross domestic product	0	0.1	0.2
Participation			
Millions of people	0	3.4	9.3
Percentage of U.S. residents	0	1.3	3.0
Average Spending per Participant (2012 dollars)	0	2,300	3,900

Source: Congressional Budget Office.

Notes: The Federal Pell Grant Program began paying benefits in 1974. The data shown here are described in Appendix A. SNAP = Supplemental Nutrition Assistance Program.

[a] Comprehensive data on participation and spending per participant are not available for the child nutrition programs.

The participation rate (the percentage of U.S. residents taking part in SNAP) grew from 5 percent in 1972 to 14 percent in 2011. The rise in participation was particularly rapid in the past decade, both before and after the recent recession began. The number of people receiving SNAP benefits increased by almost 40 percent between fiscal years 2002 and 2007 and even more rapidly, by about 60 percent, between fiscal years 2008 and 2011. Between 2002 and 2007, greater participation mainly resulted from outreach initiatives, including efforts to increase awareness of SNAP and streamline the application process. The faster rise between 2008 and 2011 occurred primarily because of poor economic conditions, although outreach efforts continued to play a role.

Average spending per SNAP participant increased from $800 to $1,800 over the 1972–2011 period, in part because SNAP benefits rise as the cost of food does and because lawmakers have changed the formula for determining the amount of benefits several times in the past 40 years. Through most of that period, per-person spending grew steadily, reaching about $1,500 in 2008. The following year, largely because of temporarily higher benefit amounts enacted in ARRA, benefits increased to roughly $1,800 per recipient; they remained near that amount through 2011.

Child Nutrition Programs

A collection of federal programs provide free or reduced-price meals, generally in schools, to children from low-income families. Those child nutrition programs include the National School Lunch Program and the School Breakfast Program, which offer meals to low-income students in kindergarten through 12th grade. Smaller child nutrition programs provide meals to children in day care or to students after school or during the summer. Federal programs of those types have existed since the 1930s but have varied in size and scope over time.[18]

Total spending on child nutrition programs grew from $3 billion in 1972 to $9 billion in 1991 and $18 billion in 2011. As a share of GDP, spending doubled—from 0.06 percent of GDP in 1972 to 0.12 percent in 2011. That growth was slower and more consistent than the growth of spending on SNAP. For example, whereas spending on SNAP shot up during the recession that began in December 2007, spending on child nutrition programs increased only modestly (see the top panel of Figure 5).

Total participation in child nutrition programs is difficult to measure because an unknown number of children take part in more than one program—for example, many children who participate in the School Breakfast Program also participate in the National School Lunch Program. For that reason, CBO could not calculate the extent to which the increase in total spending on child nutrition programs sprang from population growth, changes in participation, or changes in spending per participant.

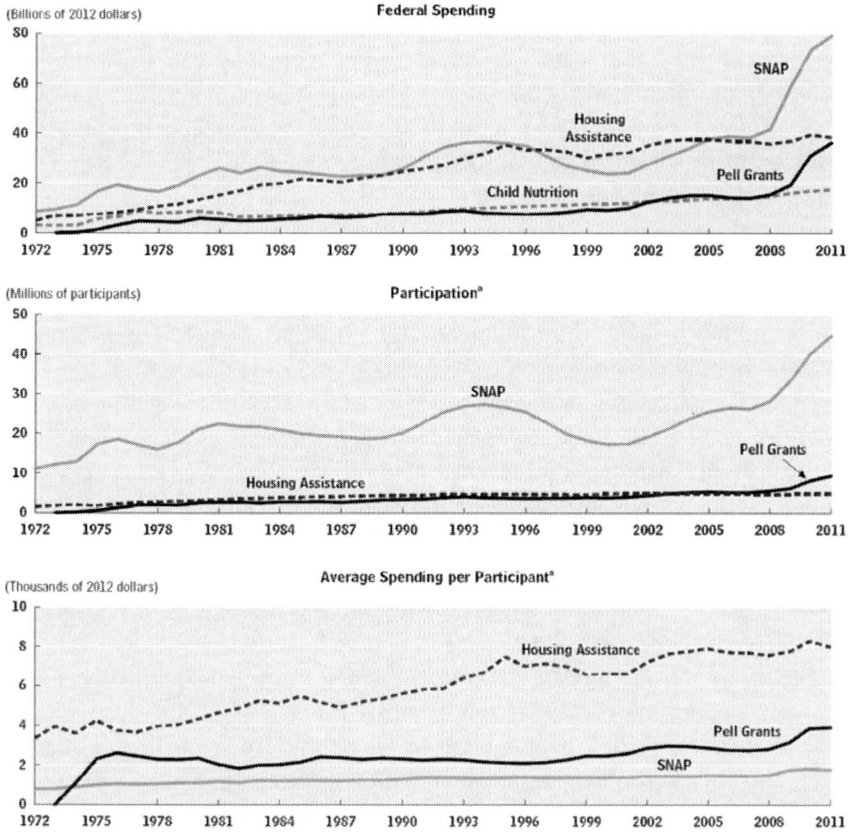

Source: Congressional Budget Office.

Notes: The data used for this figure are described in Appendix A. SNAP = Supplemental Nutrition Assistance Program.

a. For SNAP and Pell grants, participation is measured as the number of people who receive benefits. For housing assistance programs, participation is measured as the number of households that receive benefits. (Households can contain more than one person.) Comprehensive data on participation and spending per participant are not available for the child nutrition programs.

Figure 5. Growth in Selected Means-Tested Programs That Assist with Nutrition, Housing, and Education, 1972 to 2011.

Housing Programs

Several federal programs provide housing assistance to families with low income. The largest programs were authorized under section 8 of the United States Housing Act of 1937 and help people with their rent. Section 8 subsidies can take the form of vouchers that recipients can use with any landlord or specific units that are set aside for eligible recipients. In addition to the Section 8 programs, the largest of the other federal housing programs considered here subsidize capital and operating expenses for the construction of housing for low-income residents.[19]

Spending on housing assistance grew much more quickly during the first 20 years of the 1972–2011 period than during the second 20 years. Between 1972 and 1991, spending on housing assistance programs increased fivefold, from $5 billion to $26 billion (adjusted for inflation). Both the participation rate and spending per participant roughly doubled during that period. Between 1991 and 2011, spending on means-tested housing programs grew much more slowly, by about 50 percent, and remained roughly constant as a share of GDP. The growth of spending during that period was caused mostly by rising spending per participant—the amount spent per subsidized household increased from $5,800 in 1991 to $8,000 in 2011. Program participation grew only slightly during that period when measured as the number of subsidized households and fell modestly when measured as the percentage of households receiving assistance (see Table 4).

The share of the population that benefits from housing programs is noticeably smaller than the share that benefits from some of the other means-tested programs included in this analysis. In 2011, 4 percent of households participated in federal housing assistance programs, compared with about 17 percent of the population for Medicaid, 18 percent of tax filers for the EITC, and 14 percent of the population for SNAP. The availability of subsidized housing depends largely on the amount of federal funding that the housing assistance programs receive, which is determined annually through the appropriation process. Despite the relatively small percentage of the population that those programs serve, spending on them has been substantial—totaling $39 billion in 2011—because they provide a large amount of assistance per household receiving help.

Federal Pell Grant Program

Pell grants were established in 1972 and help fund tuition and expenses for post-secondary students from low-income families. Unlike federal student loans, Pell grants do not need to be repaid. The maximum Pell grant has varied over the years; in 2011, it was $5,550. Grant amounts are partly based on a student's family income; different calculations are used for dependent students, independent students, and independent students with their own dependents. Holding other factors constant, students from families with lower income receive larger Pell grants. In 2010, about 75 percent of Pell grant recipients had family income of $30,000 or less.

The first Pell grants were awarded in 1974, but the program took several years to ramp up. By 1977, it had 1.9 million recipients. Between 1977 and 2011, spending on the program grew from $5 billion to $36 billion. Seventy percent of that growth occurred over the last four years of the period, as the number of Pell grant recipients increased from 5.2 million in 2007 to 9.3 million in 2011.

Most of the rise in spending on Pell grants is attributable to growth in the participation rate. The share of U.S. residents receiving Pell grants grew by an average of about 2 percent a year between 1977 and 2007. That growth accelerated to an average of 15 percent a year between 2007 and 2011 as the share of U.S. residents receiving Pell grants rose from 1.7 percent to 3.0 percent. Some of that acceleration occurred because a rising share of the population attended college. A larger contributor, however, was an increase over the 2007–2011 period in the percentage of college enrollees receiving Pell grants. That increase stemmed from various factors, including the weak economy and recent legislative changes that raised the average size of Pell grants, eased eligibility standards, and simplified the application process, thus leading to greater participation.

Growth in spending per recipient also helped push up spending on Pell grants in the past several years. As law-makers increased the maximum Pell grant from $4,050 to $5,550 over the 2007–2011 period, the size of the average grant grew from $2,700 to $3,900. Despite that increase, the average Pell grant equals a smaller percentage of the average cost of college tuition now than it did in the 1980s.

PROJECTIONS FOR THE NEXT DECADE

If current laws do not change, federal spending on the major means-tested programs that subsidize health care will more than double, in inflation-adjusted (real) terms, between 2012 and 2023, CBO projects. That projection includes spending on premium assistance and cost-sharing subsidies for people who buy insurance through health insurance exchanges, which, under current law, will begin in 2014.

In contrast, total spending for means-tested cash assistance, nutrition, and education programs is projected to decline in real terms over the 2012–2023 period. (Unlike the other programs in this study, housing assistance programs rely on annual appropriations for all of their funding. For this report, CBO has not projected the size of those appropriations over the coming decade, which will depend on future actions by lawmakers.)[20]

In all, the rise in health care spending is expected to exceed the decline in spending on those other programs; consequently, CBO projects that total real spending on the means-tested programs and tax credits examined in this section of the report will rise from $553 billion in 2012 to $877 billion in 2023 under current law, an aver-age increase of about 4 percent a year above the rate of inflation. Not adjusted for inflation, total spending on those programs will amount to $1,076 billion in 2023, CBO projects, or about 4.2 percent of GDP. (For year-by-year details about those real and nominal projections, see Table A-2 in Appendix A.)

Means-Tested Health Care Programs and Premium Assistance Tax Credits

Under current law, federal spending on the means-tested health care programs included in this report is projected to increase substantially in real terms over the next 10 years: from $272 billion in 2012 to $624 billion in 2023. Such spending declined by about 10 percent in 2012 as states reverted to paying a larger share of Medicaid costs after the expiration of provisions in ARRA that had reduced their share. Lower federal spending for Medicaid is expected to be short-lived, however, for two main reasons. First, health care costs in general will probably continue to rise faster than inflation. Second, the Affordable Care Act will expand Medicaid eligibility, causing more people to participate in the program, and the federal government will pay a larger share of costs for newly eligible people than it pays for most people who are eligible under the current rules. As a result, CBO projects that federal spending on Medicaid will increase by 86 percent in real terms over the next decade: from $251 billion in 2012 to $467 billion in 2023 (see Figure 6).

Besides expanding Medicaid, the ACA provides for subsidies to help some low-and moderate-income people purchase health insurance through newly established insurance exchanges.

Tax filers who have income between 100 percent and 400 percent of the federal poverty guidelines and who do not have access to certain other sources of health insurance will receive a premium assistance tax credit when they buy health insurance through the exchanges. They may also receive cost-sharing subsidies, which will cover some of the out-of-pocket payments they make for health care.[21] Most of those exchange subsidies are expected to go to people with income below 200 percent of the poverty guidelines. That subsidy program is designed so that eligible people with relatively low income will receive greater benefits than those with higher income.

The health insurance exchanges are scheduled to begin operating in 2014, at which point spending on exchange subsidies—the refundable portion of the premium assistance tax credit and the cost-sharing subsidies—will amount to $18 billion (in 2012 dollars), CBO projects. (In addition, the nonrefundable portion of the tax credit is projected to reduce federal revenues by $6 billion in 2014.)

Participation in the exchanges is expected to ramp up quickly over the following years, bringing spending to $87 billion (in 2012 dollars) by 2017. Spending is projected to grow more slowly thereafter in real terms, reaching $109 billion in 2023. (The nonrefundable portion of the tax credit is projected to reduce federal revenues by $29 billion in 2023.) At that point, exchange subsidies would be the federal government's second-largest means-tested program, after Medicaid. Escalating spending for prescription drugs is expected to boost spending on the low-income subsidy for Medicare Part D, which is projected to more than double in real terms by 2023. Rising participation, because of the aging of the population, is also expected to contribute to the growth of spending for LIS.

Means-Tested Cash Assistance Programs and Tax Credits

Spending on cash assistance for disabled or elderly people through the SSI program is projected to increase from $50 billion in 2012 to $56 billion in 2023. That real increase in spending reflects population growth and the resulting boost in the number of SSI beneficiaries. The amount of cash assistance available to low-income people who are not disabled or elderly is projected to decline over the next 10 years.

Under current law, CBO projects, total real spending on the EITC, CTC, and TANF will fall from $98 billion in 2012 to $80 billion in 2023.

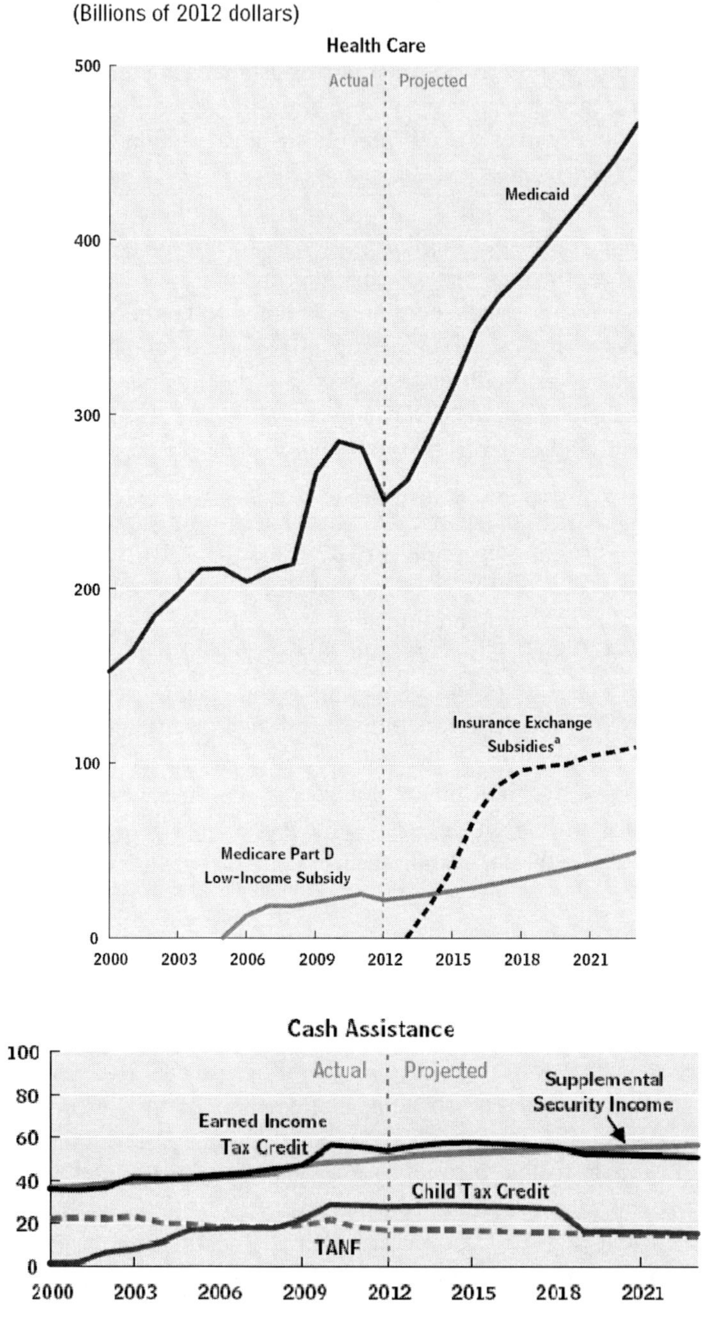
(Billions of 2012 dollars)
Health Care
Actual
Projected
Medicaid
Insurance Exchange Subsidies[a]
Medicare Part D Low-Income Subsidy
500
400
300
200
100
0
2000
2003
2006
2009
2012
2015
2018
2021
Cash Assistance
Actual
Projected
Supplemental Security Income
Earned Income Tax Credit
Child Tax Credit
TANF
100
80
60
40
20
0
2000
2003
2006
2009
2012
2015
2018
2021

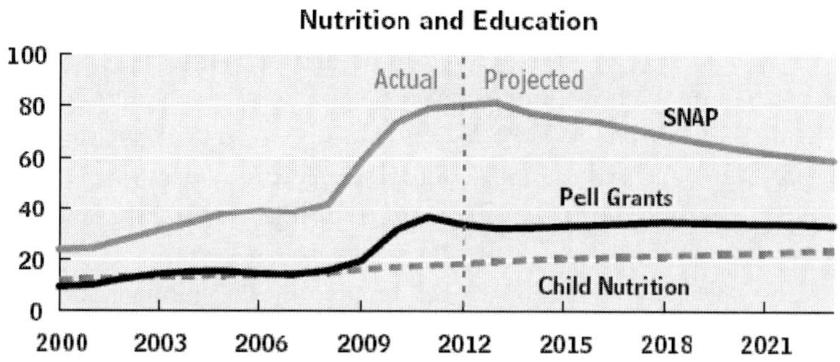

Source: Congressional Budget Office.

Notes: Numbers for tax credits consist only of amounts that are paid to tax filers because they exceed filers' tax liabilities. (In addition to those payments, the tax credits reduce federal revenues by lowering the amount that taxpayers owe.) Housing assistance programs, which are included in the historical analyses in this report, rely on annual appropriations for all of their funding. CBO has not projected the size of those appropriations, which will depend on future actions by lawmakers, so those programs are not included here. The data used for this figure are described in Appendix A. TANF = Temporary Assistance for Needy Families; SNAP = Supplemental Nutrition Assistance Program.

[a.] Subsidies for health insurance purchased through insurance exchanges, which are due to start operating in 2014, consist of refundable tax credits for premium assistance and subsidies to reduce the share of out-of-pocket costs paid by enrollees.

Figure 6. Federal Spending on Selected Means-Tested Programs and Tax Credits, 2000 to 2023.

Most of that drop involves spending on the two tax credits, because provisions of ARRA that have temporarily expanded the credits are set to expire in 2018. Largely because of that scheduled expiration, real spending on the tax credits is projected to fall from $82 billion in 2018 to $69 billion in 2019. The projected decline in real spending on cash assistance also reflects the assumption that TANF will continue to be funded at its current level of $17 billion without adjustments for inflation.

Means-Tested Nutrition and Education Programs

Spending on means-tested nutrition assistance programs is projected to fall in real terms from $99 billion in 2012 to $83 billion in 2023. That overall decline reflects two different trends: a projected decrease in spending on

SNAP and an increase in spending on child nutrition programs. Participation in SNAP is sensitive to economic conditions; hence, participation is expected to fall after 2013 as the economy improves, causing real spending on SNAP to decline from $80 billion in 2012 to $59 billion in 2023. Spending on child nutrition programs has risen steadily in real terms for the past four decades and is expected to continue to do so, reaching $24 billion in 2023, compared with $18 billion in 2012.

Spending on Pell grants depends on the amount that lawmakers set for the maximum grant each year. If that maximum stays at its current amount, spending for the program will be roughly the same in 2023 as in 2012, adjusted for inflation. Under those circumstances, the number of recipients would increase slightly.

Appendix A. Data on Means-Tested Programs and Tax Credits

The data used for this analysis come from a variety of sources and differ in numerous ways (see Table A-1). Those data share several general features, however:

- They cover only outlays by the federal government, although states have also spent large amounts on Medicaid, Aid to Families with Dependent Children (AFDC), Temporary Assistance for Needy Families (TANF), and Supplemental Security Income (SSI) over the years.
- Federal spending on administrative costs is included in the data for Medicaid, insurance exchange subsidies, AFDC, TANF, the Supplemental Nutrition Assistance Program, child nutrition programs, and housing assistance programs.
- Spending and participation are generally reported for the federal fiscal year (which begins on October 1) in which the outlays are made, with the following exceptions:
  - Data for SSI for 1974 to 1983 are reported on a calendar year basis.
  - Data for the earned income and child tax credits are reported for the fiscal year in which tax returns are due.

Table A-1. Sources of Historical Data for This Analysis

Program	Source	Notes
Health Care		
Medicaid	Spending for 1987 through 2011: Treasury Department. Additional data: Centers for Medicare & Medicaid Services, *Medicaid Financial Management Reports* (various years), the Medicaid Statistical Information System, and Form HCFA-2082 filings.	The tallies of participants include recipients in Puerto Rico and the U.S. Virgin Islands; the numbers for 2009 to 2011 are preliminary.
Medicare Part D Low-Income Subsidy	Unpublished tabulations from the Centers for Medicare & Medicaid Services.	Annual spending is based on 12 monthly payments, although 11 to 13 payment dates may fall within a year.
Cash Assistance		
Earned Income and Child Tax Credits	Internal Revenue Service, *Statistics of Income: Individual Income Tax Returns*, Publication 1304 (various years).	Eligibility for the tax credits is determined on a calendar year basis. Participation and spending are attributed to the following fiscal year because that is when most tax refunds are claimed.
Supplemental Security Income	Social Security Administration, SSI Monthly Statistics (various months), and Annual Statistical Supplement (1985).	For 1974 to 1983, spending is reported on a calendar year basis, and participation is tallied in December. For 1984 to 2011, spending is reported on a fiscal year basis, and participation is measured as a monthly average over the course of the fiscal year. Annual spending is based on 12 monthly payments, although 11 to 13 payment dates may fall within a year.

Table A-1. (Continued)

Program	Source	Notes
Aid to Families with Dependent Children (AFDC) and Temporary Assistance for Needy Families (TANF)	For 2009 and earlier: House Committee on Ways and Means, *Green Book* (2011 and 1996). For 2010 and 2011: Department of Health and Human Services, Administration for Children & Families, online archives of data and reports for TANF, http:// archive.acf.hhs.gov/programs/ ofa/data-reports/index.htm.	Spending figures for AFDC include funding for two AFDC-related programs that were also replaced by TANF: Emergency Assistance to Needy Families, and Job Opportunities and Basic Skills Training.
Nutrition, Housing, and Education		
Supplemental Nutrition Assistance Program (SNAP) and Child Nutrition Programs	For spending: Office of Management and Budget, *Budget of the U.S. Government, Fiscal Year 2013* (February 2012). For participation in SNAP: Department of Agriculture, "Supplemental Nutrition Assistance Program Participation and Costs" (December 7, 2012), www.fns.usda.gov/pd/ NAPsummary. htm.	Child nutrition programs include the National School Lunch Program, the School Breakfast Program, the Child and Adult Care Food Program, and four smaller programs.
Housing Assistance Programs	Department of Housing and Urban Development, Annotated Tables for the 2001 Budget (2001); and Congressional Research Service, Overview of Federal Housing Assistance Programs and Policy (2011).	Programs considered include rental assistance (mostly Section 8) and assistance for capital and operating expenses for public housing.
Federal Pell Grant Program	Department of Education, 2010–2011 Federal Pell Grant Program End-of-Year Report (2012).	Data are reported by the academic year for which the grants are awarded.

Source: Congressional Budget Office.

Table A-2. Projected Federal Spending on Selected Means-Tested Programs and Tax Credits in Real and Nominal Dollars

(By fiscal year)												
	Actual, 2012	**2013**	**2014**	**2015**	**2016**	**2017**	**2018**	**2019**	**2020**	**2021**	**2022**	**2023**
	Health Care											
Medicaid												
Billions of real (2012) dollars	251	262	288	316	348	367	381	396	413	429	446	467
Billions of nominal dollars	251	265	297	331	372	399	422	449	476	505	536	572
Medicare Part D Low-Income Subsidy												
Billions of real (2012) dollars	21	23	25	26	29	31	33	36	39	42	45	49
Billions of nominal dollars[a]	21	23	25	28	30	34	37	41	45	49	54	60
Insurance Exchange Subsidies												
Billions of real (2012) dollars	0	0	18	39	69	87	96	98	99	104	106	109
Billions of nominal dollars[b]	0	0	19	41	74	95	106	111	115	122	128	134
	Cash Assistance											
Earned Income and Child Tax Credits[c]												
Billions of real (2012) dollars	81	84	86	86	85	83	82	69	68	67	67	66
Billions of nominal dollars[d]	81	85	88	90	90	91	91	78	79	79	80	81
Supplemental Security Income												
Billions of real (2012) dollars	50	52	52	53	53	54	54	54	55	55	56	56
Billions of nominal dollars[e]	50	52	54	56	57	59	60	62	63	65	67	69
Temporary Assistance for Needy Families												
Billions of real (2012) dollars	17	17	17	17	16	16	16	15	15	15	14	14

Table A-2. (Continued)

	Actual, 2012	2013	2014	2015	2016	2017	2018	2019	2020	2021	2022	2023
Billions of nominal dollars	17	17	17	17	17	17	17	17	17	17	17	17
	Nutrition and Education											
Supplemental Nutrition Assistance Program												
Billions of real (2012) dollars	80	81	77	75	74	72	69	66	64	62	61	59
Billions of nominal dollars	80	82	80	79	79	78	76	75	74	73	73	73
Child Nutrition Programs												
Billions of real (2012) dollars	18	19	20	20	21	21	22	22	22	23	23	24
Billions of nominal dollars[f]	18	20	21	21	22	23	24	25	26	27	28	29
Federal Pell Grant Program[g]												
Billions of real (2012) dollars	34	32	32	33	33	34	35	34	34	34	34	33
Billions of nominal dollars	34	33	33	34	36	37	38	39	39	40	40	41

Source: Congressional Budget Office.

Note: Projections in nominal dollars reflect the value of the dollar in the year in which the spending is projected to occur and thus include the effects of inflation. Projections in real dollars reflect the value of the dollar in 2012 and thus exclude the effects of inflation. To calculate the amounts in real dollars, CBO adjusted the nominal amounts for inflation using the price index for personal consumption expenditures, which is calculated by the Bureau of Economic Analysis. The projections incorporate the assumption that current laws generally remain unchanged.

a. These amounts differ from CBO's baseline projections because they are based on 12 monthly payments per year, although 11 to 13 payments may be made within a year, depending on the calendar.

b. These are the amounts that underlie the numbers reported in Table 1-3 of CBO's Budget and Economic Outlook: Fiscal Years 2013 to 2023 ; the amounts shown in that table include the portion of exchange subsidies recorded as outlays in the federal budget and grants to help states establish insurance exchanges, but they exclude the portion of exchange subsidies that are recorded as revenues.

c. Numbers for tax credits consist only of amounts that are paid to tax filers because they exceed filers' tax liabilities.

d. To be consistent with the historical analysis presented in this report, these amounts are projected from historical data in the Internal Revenue Service's Statistics of Income database. They differ from CBO's baseline projections, which are based on amounts reported in the Treasury Department's Monthly Treasury Statement.

e. These amounts differ from CBO's baseline projections, as shown in Table 1-3 of The Budget and Economic Outlook: Fiscal Years 2013 to 2023 , because they exclude adjustments stemming from the recovery of overpayments to beneficiaries and are based on 12 monthly payments per year, although 11 to 13 payments may actually be made within a year, depending on the calendar.

f. These amounts differ from CBO's baseline projections, as shown in Table 1-3 of The Budget and Economic Outlook: Fiscal Years 2013 to 2023, because the projections in that table include the Senior Farmers' Market Nutrition Program and the Strengthening Markets, Income, and Supply account.

g. These amounts consist of both mandatory and discretionary spending for Pell grants and reflect the assumption that future maximum discretionary award levels will remain at $4,860, as set in the most recent appropriation act; they are shown by the academic year for which the grants are awarded, which begins on July 1 of the preceding calendar year.

    - Data for Pell grants are reported by the academic year for which the grants are awarded (which begins on July 1 of the preceding calendar year).
- Participation is generally measured as an average over the course of a fiscal year.

The spending figures for 2012 to 2023 in this analysis come from the Congressional Budget Office's February 2013 baseline, which was published in *The Budget and Economic Outlook: Fiscal Years 2013 to 2023* . The projections in that report are shown in nominal dollars; for the purposes of this analysis, they were adjusted for inflation and shown in 2012 dollars. In addition, for some of the programs and tax credits, those projections were adjusted to exclude shifts in the timing of certain payments and, in the case of the earned income and child tax credits, to be consistent with the historical data used for this analysis (see Table A-2).

APPENDIX B. INTERPRETING INFORMATION ABOUT PARTICIPATION AND SPENDING PER PARTICIPANT

In general, the participation figures given for various means-tested programs and tax credits in this report represent the average number of recipients per month in a particular year.

"Participant" means different things in different programs, however. For Medicaid, the Medicare Part D low-income subsidy, the Supplemental Nutrition Assistance Program (SNAP), Supplemental Security Income, and Pell grants, the number of participants is the number of individuals who receive benefits. (That figure is lower than the number of people who are eligible for a program.) For the earned income and child tax credits, the number of participants is the number of tax-filing units (as measured by tax returns) that receive refundable credits. Tax-filing units can include more than one person.

For housing assistance programs, the number of participants is the number of households receiving benefits, as approximated by the number of subsidized units available to households. (Households can also include more than one person.) For Temporary Assistance for Needy Families (TANF) or the child nutrition programs, available data do not provide a reliable measure of the number of participants.

Several caveats apply to the information about participation and spending per participant that the Congressional Budget Office (CBO) used for this analysis:

- The number of participants in each program or tax credit cannot be added together to estimate the total number of people participating in at least one of the programs, because some people receive benefits from more than one program at a given time.[22]
- Figures for average spending per participant in various programs cannot be added together to estimate how much a typical participant receives in means-tested benefits over the course of a year, because very few people participate in all of the programs included in this report.
- Average spending per participant does not represent the benefit amount that every recipient receives. Even within a program, benefits generally differ among participants. For example, Medicaid spending per participant is much higher for people who are elderly, disabled, or pregnant than it is for nondisabled children or for working-age adults who are not disabled or pregnant.

End Notes

[1] For ease of presentation, this report frequently uses the term "programs" to encompass both the spending programs and the tax credits.

[2] The Affordable Care Act comprises the Patient Protection and Affordable Care Act and the health care provisions of the Health Care and Education Reconciliation Act of 2010.

[3] For another recent analysis of means-tested programs and tax credits, see Gene Falk, *Low-Income Assistance Programs: Trends in Federal Spending,* Report for Congress R41823 (Congressional Research Service, June 13, 2012).

[4] For more information about such tax expenditures, see Congressional Budget Office, *The Budget and Economic Outlook: Fiscal Years 2012 to 2022* (January 2012), pp. 93–96, www.cbo.gov/publication/42905 .

[5] Growth in participation and growth in spending per participant interact in ways that push program spending higher than it would be without such interactions. The interaction between those factors can be identified separately, or, as in this analysis, equal portions of the interaction can be attributed to each factor.

[6] In addition, the Children's Health Insurance Program (CHIP), which was established by the Balanced Budget Act of 1997, insured about 5 million low-income people in 2011 who were not eligible for Medicaid. CHIP is means-tested, but with spending of $9 billion in 2011, it was smaller than the programs included in this report.

[7] Some of those proportions are expected to shift as the Affordable Care Act is implemented. For instance, CBO estimates that by 2020, people who are elderly or disabled will account for about one-fifth of Medicaid enrollment and just over half of the program's spending.

[8] Some changes to covered services have also had the effect of increasing Medicaid enrollment. As services that targeted particular populations were added, enrollment among those populations increased. Other policy changes extended new benefits to new populations. For example, the Medicare Catastrophic Coverage Act of 1988 was the first of several laws that required state Medic-aid programs to pay the cost-sharing amounts—and in some cases the Medicare premiums—of low-income Medicare beneficiaries.

[9] See, for example, Richard G. Frank, Howard H. Goldman, and Michael Hogan, "Medicaid and Mental Health: Be Careful What You Ask For," *Health Affairs,* vol. 22, no. 1 (January 2003), pp. 101–113, http://dx.doi.org/10.1377/hlthaff.22.1.101 .

[10] The federal poverty guidelines issued by the Department of Health and Human Services, which are used to determine eligibility for various programs, differ slightly from the poverty thresholds issued by the Census Bureau, which are used mainly for statistical purposes (such as determining the number of people living in poverty). For a family of two, eligibility for LIS required a family income of less than about $22,000 in 2011; for more information, see Congressional Budget Office, *Spending Patterns for Prescription Drugs Under Medicare Part D* (December 2011), www.cbo.gov/publication/42692 .

[11] For more information about those and other tax credits, see Congressional Budget Office, *Refundable Tax Credits* (January 2013), www.cbo.gov/publication/43767 .

[12] SSI benefits are not reduced for the receipt of in-kind benefits, such as nutrition, housing, or education assistance. For more information about the SSI program and options for changing it, see Congressional Budget Office, *Supplemental Security Income: An Overview* (December 2012), www.cbo.gov/publication/43759 .

[13] 493 U.S. 521, 541 (1990).

[14] By law, the maximum monthly SSI benefit increases with the cost of living as measured by the consumer price index for urban wage earners and clerical workers (CPI-W). In converting dollar amounts to 2012 dollars to remove the effects of inflation for this analysis, CBO measured inflation using the PCE price index, which accounts more fully than the CPI-W does for consumers' ability to purchase cheaper goods when they become available. Neither the PCE price index nor the CPI-W specifically measures the cost of living for disabled or elderly people.

[15] Spending figures for AFDC include funding for two AFDC-related programs that were also replaced by TANF: Emergency Assistance to Needy Families, and Job Opportunities and Basic Skills Training.

[16] Funding for the program each year is set by law. The statutory authorization for TANF expired in 2010, and the program has been maintained through a series of short-term extensions since then.

[17] For a more complete discussion of the program and options for changing it, see Congressional Budget Office, *The Supplemental Nutrition Assistance Program* (April 2012), www.cbo.gov/publication/43173 .

[18] See Gordon W. Gunderson, *The National School Lunch Program: Background and Development* (Department of Agriculture, 1971), www.fns.usda.gov/cnd/lunch/AboutLunch/ProgramHistory.htm .

[19] For more information about housing assistance programs, see Congressional Budget Office, *An Overview of Federal Support for Housing* (November 2009), www.cbo.gov/publication/41219 .

[20] Appropriations for the housing programs are subject to automatic spending cuts under the Budget Control Act of 2011. The other programs and tax credits analyzed in this report are largely not subject to those cuts, but the cuts do apply to some smaller means-tested programs that are not included here, such as the Special Supplemental Nutrition Program for Women, Infants, and Children (known as WIC).

[21] For CBO's most recent estimates of the costs of subsidies provided under the ACA, see Congressional Budget Office, *The Budget and Economic Outlook: Fiscal Years 2013 to 2023* (February 2013), Appendix A, www.cbo.gov/publication/43907 .

[22] In an analysis of Medicaid, SNAP, TANF, and the Children's Health Insurance Program (which is not included in this report), CBO determined that about 45 percent of the low-income families who received assistance from at least one of those programs participated in multiple programs, although only about 3 percent of them participated in all four programs. See Congressional Bud-get Office, *Effective Marginal Tax Rates for Low- and Moderate-Income Workers* (November 2012), www.cbo.gov/publication/ 43709 .

In: Means-Tested Programs ... ISBN: 978-1-62618-552-4
Editors: E. B. White and C. C. Mitchell © 2013 Nova Science Publishers, Inc.

Chapter 2

LOW-INCOME ASSISTANCE PROGRAMS: TRENDS IN FEDERAL SPENDING*

Gene Falk

SUMMARY

This report examines the spending trends of 10 major need-tested benefit programs or groups of programs: (1) health care from Medicaid and the Children's Health Insurance Program (CHIP); (2) the refundable portion of the health insurance tax credit enacted in the 2010 health care reform law; (3) the Supplemental Nutrition Assistance Program (SNAP); (4) assisted housing; (5) financial assistance for post-secondary students (Pell Grants); (6) compensatory education grants to school districts; (7) the Earned Income Tax Credit (EITC); (8) the Additional Child Tax Credit (ACTC); (9) Supplemental Security Income (SSI); and (10) Family Support Payments. The common feature of need-tested programs is that they provide benefits, services, or funding based on a measure of limited financial resources (income and sometimes assets). However, other than that common feature, the programs differ considerably in their target populations, services, and focus.

In total and in inflation-adjusted terms, federal outlays for major need-tested programs increased in each decade examined in this report, from the 1960s to the present. There have been particularly large increases in need-

* This is an edited, reformatted and augmented version of the Congressional Research Service Publication, CRS Report for Congress R41823, dated June 13, 2012.

tested outlays during recent years, attributable to the effects of the recession (which increased the number of people eligible for aid) and policy responses to it that increased federal funding and benefits for certain programs. The Congressional Budget Office (CBO) forecasts that under current law, federal outlays for need-tested programs would continue to increase, even in inflation-adjusted terms, in the upcoming decade. However, that increase is attributable to health care programs. For programs other than health care, total inflation-adjusted spending is projected to decrease over the period FY2011 through FY2022. CBO forecasts that with the economic recovery, caseload increases in certain programs will abate. Additionally, most of the policy responses to the recession were temporary in nature. Different programs also have different spending trends. Cash benefits—to needy families with dependent children and the aged, blind, and disabled—comprised most aid to low-income families in the early 1960s. However, over the period from the 1960s through the end of the 1980s, most of the growth in aid was for non-cash benefits in the form of education, food, housing, and medical assistance.

The 1990s was the decade of "welfare reform." The policies affecting low-income families with children, in particular, were substantially altered, with less emphasis on providing a "safety net" for families without a worker and more emphasis on aiding low-income workers in a system geared to "make work pay." Spending on need-tested aid, even excluding health care, increased in the decade of the 1990s. Federal funding for cash assistance for needy families with children fell, but this was far more than offset by increases in the EITC, which supplements the earnings of lower-income families, as well as federal funding for other programs that support lower-earning families (e.g., child care subsidies). Relative to the size of the economy, aggregate need-tested aid has generally increased since the 1960s. The 4.2% of the Gross Domestic Product (GDP) accounted for by these programs in FY2011 compares with 3.0% of GDP in FY2007, 2.7% of GDP in FY2000, and 2.0% of GDP in FY1990. CBO projects that, under current law, total need-tested aid will first fall but then increase as a share of GDP, again reaching about 4.2% of GDP in 2016 and 2022. However, all projected growth in spending as a share of GDP is from the health programs.

INTRODUCTION

The high current and projected federal budget deficits, and debate over the size and scope of federal spending, have raised interest in how federal dollars are spent. This report focuses on federal outlays for major "need-tested" programs—programs targeted toward families and individuals with limited income. The major need-tested programs discussed in this report provide cash, food, housing, and medical assistance to families and individuals with limited financial resources with collective FY2011 federal outlays of $622 billion. These programs represented 16.5% of all federal outlays and 4.2% of the Gross Domestic Product (GDP).

This report provides perspective on current federal outlays for these programs, examining historical trends in their federal outlays as well as showing the Congressional Budget Office's (CBO's) March 2012 baseline budget projections for them.

The baseline projections cover the period from FY2012 through FY2022. The baseline budget projections indicate what spending would be if current law were continued. Additional perspective is provided by showing their trends as a percentage of all federal outlays as well as a percent of GDP.

NEED-TESTED PROGRAMS

The common feature of need-tested programs is that they provide benefits, services, or funding based on a measure of low financial resources (income and sometimes assets). However, other than that common feature, the programs differ considerably in their target populations, benefits, services, and focus.

That is, aid from these programs is not provided to one group of people or families, nor do these programs address the same purpose. Some address basic needs (food, housing, and medical care); others (e.g., student financial assistance) seek to enable recipients to overcome financial need in order to engage in an activity.

Moreover, need-tested programs are not the only programs that benefit low-income persons and families. More universally available social programs, such as the social insurance programs of Social Security, Medicare, and Unemployment Insurance or programs such as Guaranteed Student Loans, also benefit low-income persons and families. These programs also tend to be substantially larger (in spending) than need-based programs.

To simplify the analysis, this report focuses on nine of the largest need-tested programs (based on federal outlays) in FY2011 plus subsidies for health care that were created in the 2010 health reform law, and are available to lower-income families and persons.[1]

The need-tested programs included in this report are the following:[2]

- **Medicaid/CHIP.** Medicaid provides medical assistance to needy families with dependent children and the aged, blind, and disabled who have low incomes. Beginning in 2014, states will be required to expand coverage to able-bodied individuals under age 65 with incomes below 133% of the federal poverty guidelines. A large share of Medicaid expenditures pays for nursing home care for the elderly and disabled. The State Children's Health Insurance Program (CHIP) allows states to cover targeted low-income children with no health insurance in families with income above Medicaid eligibility levels. In addition, when certain conditions are met, states may extend CHIP coverage to pregnant women and parents of Medicaid and CHIP-eligible children. In FY2011, Medicaid/CHIP outlays of $284 billion accounted for 7.9% of all federal outlays and 1.9% of GDP.
- **The health insurance tax credit**, created by the 2010 health care reform law,[3] will help certain individuals and families purchase health insurance beginning in 2014. Under the 2010 health reform law, individuals and families not otherwise covered will be able to purchase health insurance from state-based "exchanges." Families with incomes below 400% of the poverty line will have their out-of-pocket premium payments capped at a certain percentage of their incomes.[4] The remainder of the premium cost would be paid for through an advance-payable, refundable tax credit. The refundable portion of that tax credit is considered a federal outlay.
- **Supplemental Nutrition Assistance Program (SNAP, the program formerly known as food stamps)** provides low-income families with an income supplement to enable them to purchase a minimal cost, nutritious diet. SNAP is available to all low-income households regardless of their demographic composition, though benefits for able-bodied adults without dependents and who are not working is time-limited and certain noncitizens are excluded.[5] SNAP benefits are uniform nationwide for families of a given size except in Alaska, Hawaii, and the territories. In FY2011, SNAP outlays of $78 billion accounted for 2.2% of all federal outlays and 0.5% of GDP.
- **Student Financial Assistance**, mostly Pell Grants, provides funds to students from low-income families to help meet the cost of post-secondary education. Awards are based on a need analysis that considers both the cost of education and financial resources of the

student's family. In FY2011, outlays for student financial assistance of $38 billion accounted for 1.1% of all federal outlays and 0.3% of GDP.

- **Compensatory Education** (Title I-A of the Elementary and Secondary Education Act) provides aid to school districts based on their number and percentage of economically disadvantaged children. The purpose of this aid is to ensure that each child has a high-quality education and reaches, at a minimum, proficiency on state academic achievement standards and assessments under the No Child Left Behind Act. In FY2011, total outlays for compensatory education grants of $19.5 billion accounted for 0.5% of all federal outlays and 0.1% of GDP.
- **Housing Assistance**, as categorized for this report, includes federal outlays for project-based rental assistance and tenant-based vouchers (under the Section 8 program); other support for public housing; and housing assistance for the elderly, the disabled, and American Indians. In FY2011, housing assistance outlays of $40 billion accounted for 1.1% of all federal outlays and 0.3% of GDP.
- **The Earned Income Tax Credit (EITC)** represents the refundable portion of the earned income tax credit. It provides an earnings supplement for low-wage earners, with the size of the credit dependent on family type and earnings. The bulk of EITC dollars goes to families with children. Historically, the bulk of refundable EITC dollars was delivered through tax refund checks. Beginning in 2012, all "advance payments" of EITC benefits are ended, and all refundable EITC dollars will be paid through refund checks. In FY2011, EITC outlays of $56 billion accounted for 1.5% of all federal outlays and 0.4% of GDP.
- **The Additional Child Tax Credit (ACTC)** represents the refundable portion of the child tax credit. It assists eligible parents of children who have earned income above a certain threshold but whose tax liability is too small to fully benefit from the regular non-refundable child tax credit. It is delivered to families through refund checks when they file their taxes. In FY2011, ACTC outlays of $23 billion accounted for 0.6% of all federal outlays and 0.2% of GDP.
- **Supplemental Security Income (SSI)** provides a federally funded cash income floor for low-income persons or couples who are aged, blind, or disabled. Federal SSI benefits are based on uniform nationwide eligibility and benefit rules, and they are paid with federal

funds. States may supplement SSI with their own funds. InFY2011, SSI outlays of $56.5 billion accounted for 1.6% of all federal outlays and0.4% of GDP.

- **Family Support,** as categorized for this report, includes outlays for the Temporary Assistance for Needy Families (TANF) block grant, the Child Support Enforcement (CSE) program, and federal grants to help support state child care subsidy programs. In FY2011, family support outlays of $28.4 billion accounted for 0.8% of all federal outlays and 0.2% of GDP.

This report focuses only on federal outlays. A number of programs (Medicare, SNAP, housing assistance, and family support) are actually administered at the state or local level. States also contribute financially to Medicaid, SNAP (administrative and employment and training costs), and family support. Further, the bulk of financing for elementary and secondary education represents state and local dollars.

Additionally, this report focuses on programs classified as "major" by their current spending level. This focus might leave out some programs that historically comprised a greater share of aid to low-income persons. For example, employment and training programs had much higher spending levels in the 1970s than they do today.

Excluding such programs has the effect of somewhat depressing historical spending levels (in the late 1970s) and overstating growth since then. It also leaves out the part of the story regarding low-income assistance: training and employment, particularly public service employment in the late 1970s, were once a greater part of low-income aid.

Low-Income Assistance Spending Trends

Federal outlays for low-income assistance have generally, and fairly steadily, increased over the past five decades. In total, spending for low-income assistance in inflation-adjusted terms has been higher at the end of each decade. Growth in aggregate federal outlays for low-income assistance has occurred during both economic downturns and periods of economic growth.

Figure 1 shows federal outlays for the major low-income assistance programs in inflation-adjusted terms historically for FY1962 through FY2011, and shows CBO-projected outlays under current law for FY2012 through

FY2022. The figure shows several periods of pronounced growth, with the most recent occurring from FY2007 through FY2011. This represents spending, both automatic (through increased enrollment) as well as legislated (e.g., benefit and funding increases through the American Recovery and Reinvestment Act of 2009, ARRA, P.L. 111-5), in response to the deep recession from 2007-2009.

CBO baseline projections show that, under current policies, total spending on low-income assistance programs will decline in FY2012 from a peak in FY2011.

Spending, however, will again begin to increase in FY2013. However, almost all of the increases in future low-income assistance spending are attributable to spending increases for health care.

(In billions of constant FY2011 dollars)

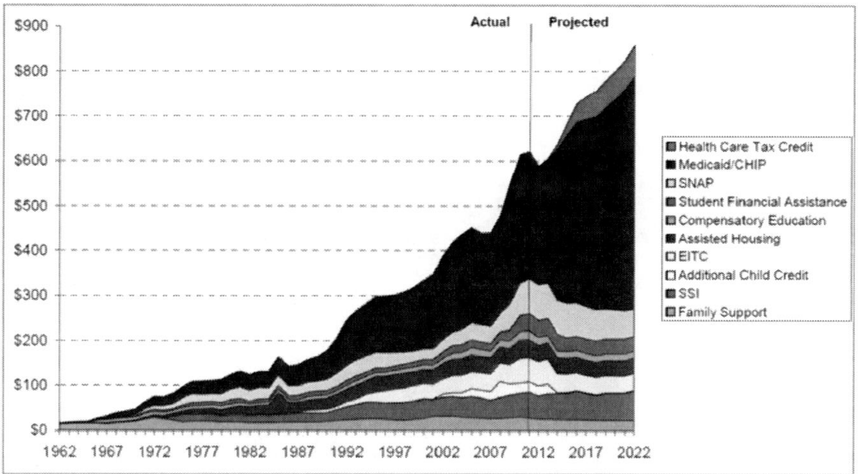

Source: Congressional Research Service (CRS), based on data from the U.S. Office of Management and Budget FY2013 Public Budget Database, and the Congressional Budget Office March 2013 baseline budget projections for FY2012 through FY2022.

Notes: Constant dollars were computed using the implicit price deflator for Gross Domestic Product (GDP).

Figure 1. Federal Outlays for Selected Low-Income Assistance Programs: FY1962 through FY2022.

Table 1. Average Annual Rate of Change in Inflation-Adjusted Outlays for Major Low-Income Assistance Programs: Selected Periods from FY1962 through FY2022

	Total	Health Programs	Non-health Programs
1962-1970	14.7%	46.5%	10.7%
1970-1980	9.8	9.8	9.8
1980-1990	3.7	6.8	2.3
1990-2000	6.5	8.9	4.9
2000-2007	4.1	4.7	3.5
2007-2011	9.0	7.8	10.0
2011-2022	3.0	6.9	-2.0

Source: Congressional Research Service (CRS), based on data from the U.S. Office of Management and Budget, FY2013 Public Budget Database, and the Congressional Budget Office, March 2012 baseline budget projections for FY2011 through FY2022.

Notes: Constant dollars were computed using the implicit price deflator for Gross Domestic Product (GDP).

Rates of Growth: Health Programs and Non-health Programs

Historically, spending for health care (mostly Medicaid) has grown faster than the other categories of low-income assistance spending. Over the entire FY1962 through FY2011 period, federal outlays for low-income health programs have increased, in inflation-adjusted terms, at a rate of 13.3% per year versus 6.5% for other spending.

Some of this is attributable to high rates of growth early in the period, as Medicaid was established.

As shown in **Table 1**, the growth of inflation-adjusted spending for health care generally outpaced the growth for other low-income assistance programs. The major exceptions were in the 1970s, when rates of growth were equivalent between health and non-health programs, and the recent recessionary period, which saw more rapid growth for non-health programs than for health programs. **Table 1** also shows that under current policies, CBO projects that health outlays would grow at an average annual rate of 6.9% in the upcoming decade, versus a decline in real spending for other low-income assistance at an average annual rate of 2.0% for that same period. The factors affecting spending for low-income health care (primarily through Medicaid) are complex. However, two major factors are

- health care cost increases that are greater than the rate of general price inflation; and
- the growth in Medicaid enrollment.

Originally, Medicaid eligibility was tied to the receipt of cash assistance from programs for the elderly, blind, and disabled and families with dependent children. Growth in the enrollment of these programs—particularly in two periods (the late 1960s through the 1970s, and the late 1980s through the early 1990s)—contributed to Medicaid spending increases. However, Medicaid enrollment also increased as a result of legislated expansions of coverage for children beyond those in families receiving cash assistance, as well as pregnant women with incomes below 133% of the federal poverty level. The much faster rate of growth in health care than in other forms of need-tested aid means that health has been an increasing share of total federal outlays for need-tested programs. **Figure 2** shows the composition of federal outlays on major low-income assistance programs for FY1962 through FY2022.

In FY1962, most need-tested aid was in the form of cash public assistance through grants to states for families with children and the aged, blind, and disabled. This has changed dramatically over time. Non-cash benefits or services, particularly health care, accounted for an increasing share of aid to low-income families and persons. In FY2011, federal outlays for Medicaid and CHIP alone accounted for almost half (46%) of all federal outlays for major low-income assistance programs. As projected under current policies by CBO, federal outlays for health will account for a growing share of need-tested aid in the coming decade. By FY2022, health would account for close to 7 out of every 10 dollars on major low-income assistance programs. The projected health outlays include the estimated costs of the expansions made in the 2010 health reform law, including the expansion of Medicaid coverage for currently uncovered persons under age 65 with incomes below 133% of the federal poverty level and the refundable portion of the health tax credit that will subsidize health insurance purchased through state exchanges for those with incomes under 400% of the federal poverty level.

Trends in Non-health Spending

The large growth in health spending obscures some of the trends in the non-health portion of aid to low-income families and persons. As discussed above, inflation-adjusted outlays for the major low-income assistance programs also grew over the past five decades, albeit at a slower rate of growth than health spending. **Figure 3** shows the trends for inflation-adjusted outlays of the selected non-health programs that provide low-income assistance. Historically, aggregate outlays for the non-health need-tested programs increased during periods of both economic downturn and economic growth. However, CBO projects that, under current law, spending for all of these programs except SSI will decline in real terms over the next few years as the economy continues to recover from the 2007-2009 recession.

Trends through the Late 1980s

As discussed above, cash benefits (in the family support category) dominated spending in the early years. Supplemental Security Income (SSI) represented a federalization of cash benefits for the aged, blind, and disabled beginning in FY1974. However, from the mid-1970s through the end of the 1980s, cash benefits as represented by the family support and SSI categories increased only slightly. The largest growth in spending through the late 1980s was in noncash benefits and services:

- **Elementary and Secondary Education Aid.** Compensatory education grants to school districts (Title I-A of the Elementary and Secondary Education Act), based on their number and percentage of disadvantaged children, date back to President Lyndon Johnson's Great Society.
- **Higher Education Aid.** The Basic Educational Opportunity Grants (BEOG), the predecessor to Pell Grants, were created in the Education Amendments of 1972.
- **SNAP (the program formerly known as food stamps).** A Food Stamp pilot program began in 1961 and legislation in 1964 made the program permanent. However, it did not operate nationwide until 1974.
- **Housing assistance.** Federal housing aid dates back to the Great Depression. Until the Housing Act of 1974, federal policy emphasized supporting the construction of public housing for low-income persons. The 1974 act established the Section 8 program, which changed the emphasis of housing assistance policies toward providing rent subsidies for lower-income households in private market housing.[6]

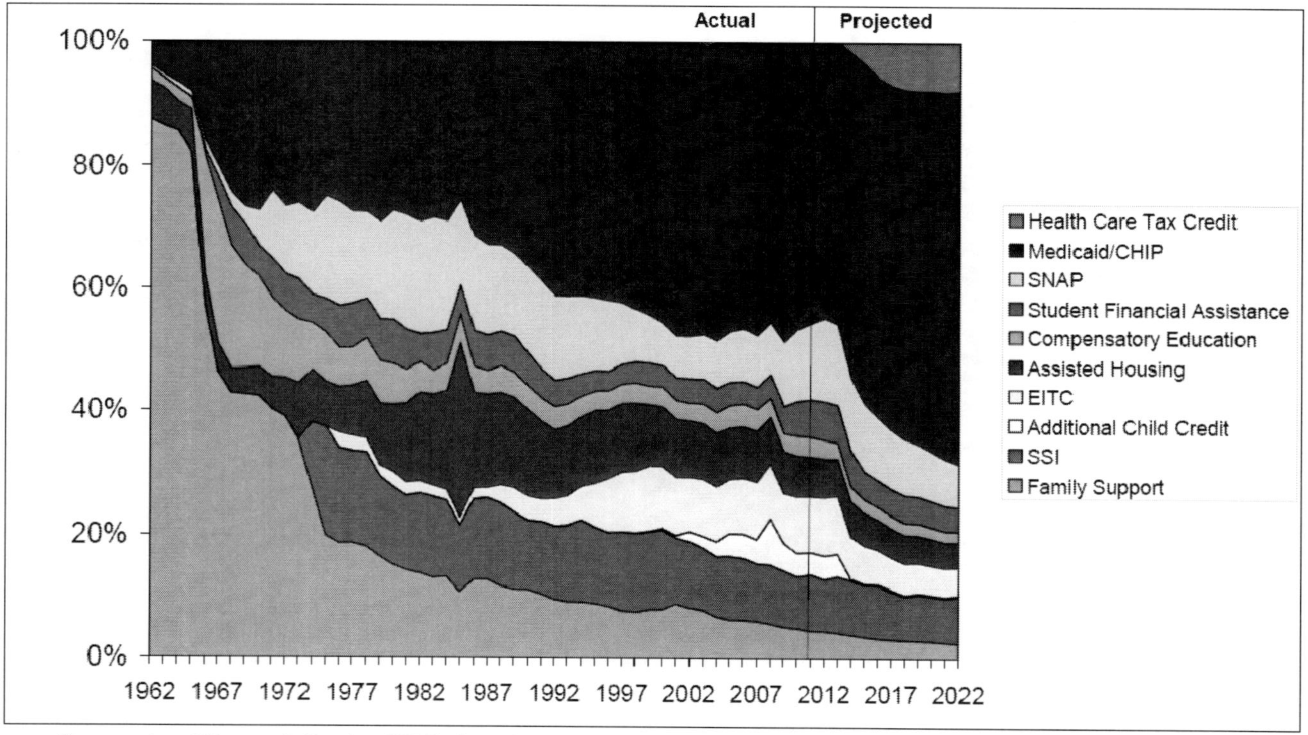

Source: Congressional Research Service (CRS), based on data from the U.S. Office of Management and Budget FY2013 Public Budget Database, and the Congressional Budget Office March 2012 baseline budget projections for FY2012 through FY2022.

Figure 2. Composition of Federal Outlays on Major Low-Income Assistance Programs: FY1962 through FY2022.

(In billions of constant FY2011 dollars)

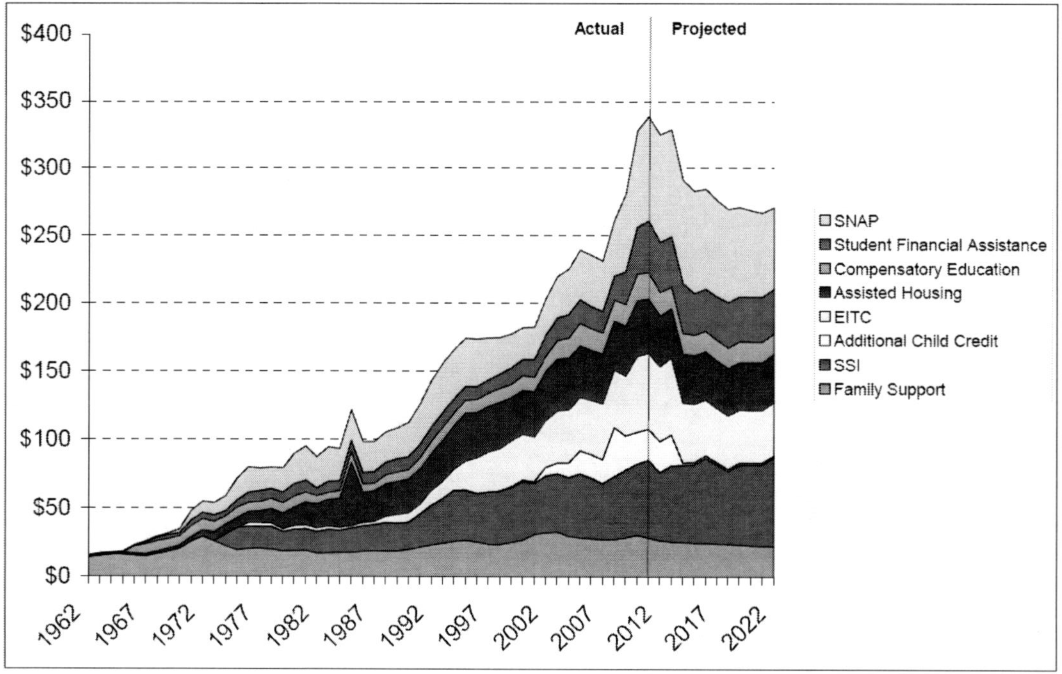

Source: Congressional Research Service (CRS), based on data from the U.S. Office of Management and Budget FY2013 Public Budget Database, and the Congressional Budget Office March 2012 baseline budget projections for FY2012 through FY2022.

Notes: Constant dollars were computed using the implicit price deflator for Gross Domestic Product (GDP).

Figure 3. Federal Outlays for Selected Non-health Low-Income Assistance Programs: FY1962 through FY2022.

The 1990s

The 1990s was the decade of welfare reform. In that decade, total spending on non-health low-income assistance programs *increased*. However, aid was substantially restructured during the period. For low-income families with children, policies were shifted away from providing a safety net for families without earnings toward a policy to support work among low-income parents. The 1996 welfare reform law converted the cash assistance entitlement for families with dependent children into the Temporary Assistance for Needy Families (TANF) block grant, with recipients of cash aid subject to work requirements and time limits for federal aid. The 1996 law also curtailed aid to noncitizens.

However, aid to working poor families with children was increased during the 1990s. Earnings supplements for working parents through the EITC were substantially expanded through legislation in 1990, with a major increase in the credit amount enacted in 1993. A child tax credit of $500 per child was established by tax legislation in 1997. The 1996 welfare reform law also substantially expanded funding to help states pay for child care subsidies for working parents.

2000-2007

The major legislated expansions in aid in the 2000s before the onset of the recession were in the EITC and child tax credit. Several pieces of legislation increased the size of the child tax credit (to $1,000 beginning in 2003). In addition, tax legislation through this period made the credit refundable to more families.[7] In addition, substantial changes were made to Pell Grants in 2007 amendments (and again in 2010).

Recent Years

There were large increases in spending for low-income aid in recent years in response to the 2007-2009 recession. This resulted from both automatic factors (increases in enrollments in the entitlement programs) as well as legislated changes. The American Recovery and Reinvestment Act of 2009 (P.L. 111-5) provided an increase in the EITC for families with three or more children; further expanded the availability of the refundable portion of the child credit; increased the average SNAP benefit by 15%; increased the maximum Pell Grant; and provided extra funding for both compensatory education and TANF.

Many of the ARRA provisions are temporary, with funding increases that have expired or are (in the case of SNAP) scheduled to expire. Additionally, the child credit (and its refundable portion, the ACTC) is scheduled to revert back to pre-2001 rules after 2012. CBO's March 2012 baseline projects that enrollment in SNAP will gradually decline as the economy recovers over the next decade. Thus, federal outlays for the major non-health need-tested programs are projected to decline, in real terms, over the coming decade.

FEDERAL OUTLAYS FOR LOW-INCOME ASSISTANCE PROGRAMS AS A PERCENT OF THE GROSS DOMESTIC PRODUCT

Federal outlays for major low-income assistance programs measured as a percent of Gross Domestic Product (GDP) provide a sense of how large these programs are relative to the size of the national economy. These programs have grown as a share of GDP over the past five decades, ending each decade at a higher level as a percent of GDP.

Figure 4 shows federal outlays for major low-income programs as a percent of GDP for FY1962 through FY2011, and as projected under the CBO baseline for FY2012 through FY2022. Outlays for these programs—both the non-health and health programs—generally increased as a share of GDP with some fluctuations due mostly to the economic cycle (e.g., increasing as a share of GDP during economic slumps, decreasing during periods of growth). The longest period of decline as a percent of GDP was in the late 1990s. Federal outlays for major low-income assistance programs as a percent of GDP decreased for four consecutive years. During this period, outlay growth for these programs increased, but at a rate slower than overall economic growth.

In FY2010 and FY2011, federal outlays on low-income assistance as a percentage of GDP reached 4.2%. Given the projected rate of growth in the economy and the continuation of current law, federal outlays for these programs would drop as a percent of GDP to 3.9% in FY2012—still higher than the pre-recession level of 3.0% of GDP in FY2007. Aggregate federal outlays for these programs are projected to increase again through FY2022, again reaching 4.2% in FY2022. However, all of that increase reflects the continued growth of health care. Federal outlays for the major non-health programs as a percent of GDP would drop from their peak 2.3% of GDP in FY2011 to below their pre-recession level by FY2017, with continued declines thereafter.

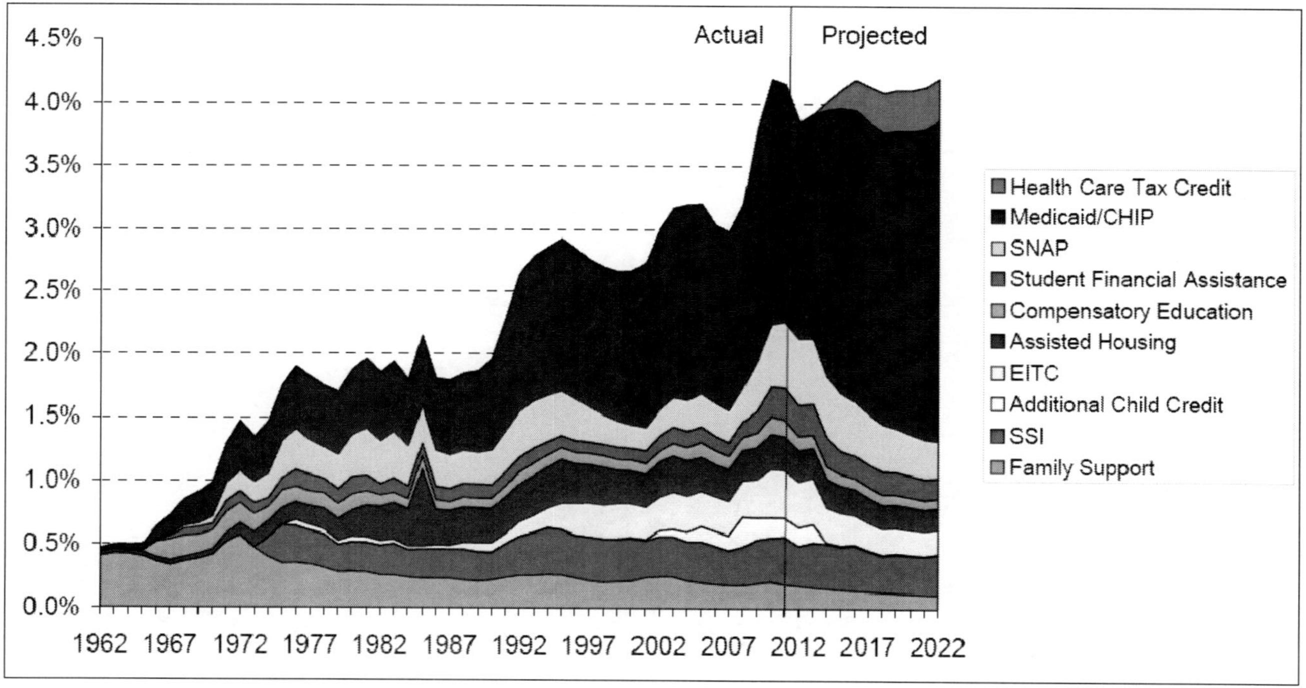

Source: Congressional Research Service (CRS), based on data from the U.S. Office of Management and Budget FY2013 Public Budget Database, and the Congressional Budget Office March 2012 baseline budget projections for FY2012 through FY2022.

Figure 4. Federal Outlays for Major Low-Income Programs as a Percent of Gross Domestic Product: FY1962 through FY2022.

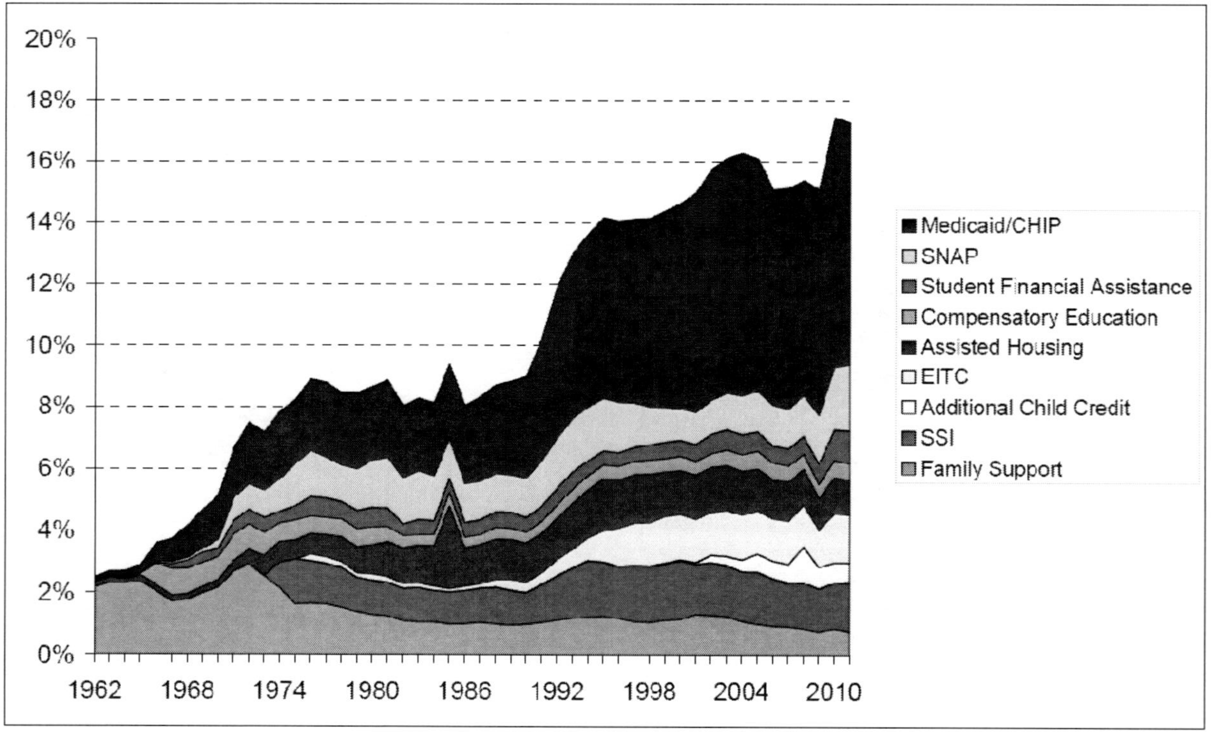

Source: Congressional Research Service (CRS), based on data from the U.S. Office of Management and Budget FY2013 Public Budget Database, and the Congressional Budget Office March 2012 baseline budget projections for FY2012 through FY2022.

Figure 5. Federal Outlays for Major Low-Income Assistance Programs as a Percent of Total Federal Outlays: FY1962 through FY2011.

FEDERAL OUTLAYS FOR LOW-INCOME ASSISTANCE PROGRAMS AS A PERCENT OF THE FEDERAL BUDGET

Though federal spending for major low-income assistance programs has increased by almost any measure, so has total federal spending. **Figure 5** shows total federal outlays for major need-tested programs as a percent of total federal spending. Though the long-term trend has been for the major need-tested programs to account for a greater share of total federal spending, the largest jumps in this measure occurred from the mid-1980s to the mid-1990s, when spending for them jumped from about 8% to 14% of total federal outlays. Aggregate federal outlays for these programs increased again to about 16% of total federal outlays by FY2004, fell before the recession, and then increased to 17.4% of total outlays in FY2010. In FY2011, federal outlays for low-income assistance programs fell slightly, to 17.3% of total outlays.

Unlike other charts in this report, **Figure 5** shows only historical spending trends for low-income assistance programs as a percent of total federal outlays. This is because the CBO current law baseline reflects the effect of automatic spending cuts due in January 2013 under the Budget Control Act of 2011 (P.L. 112-25) for total federal spending, but generally not for individual programs except for defense and Medicare spending. Most low-income assistance programs discussed in this report are exempt from these automatic cuts. The major exceptions are compensatory education grants to school districts and housing assistance programs that, under current law, are subject to automatic cuts.[8] The inconsistent treatment in the CBO current law baseline of the automatic cuts for total outlays and some of the programs discussed in this report would slightly distort an analysis of projected low-income assistance programs spending as a percent of total federal outlays. Therefore, such an analysis was excluded from this report.

CONCLUSION

At the beginning of the period examined in this report (FY1962), federal aid to address low income was dominated by grants to the states to provide public assistance for the aged, blind, and disabled and families with dependent children. Grant-in-aid programs for the low-income aged, families with dependent children, and the blind were established by the Social Security Act of 1935 and focused on groups that, during that era, were not expected to work. A grant-in-aid program for low-income disabled persons was added in 1950.

The period since the 1960s saw large changes in programs that assist low-income families. First, there were large expansions in non-cash medical, food, and housing assistance. The Great Society era also produced expanded educational aid for elementary and secondary education for school districts with large concentrations of low-income children, and the early 1970s saw the establishment of grants to help students from low-income families attend college.

Second, there was the increasing dominance of medical assistance in spending for low-income families. By FY2011, Medicaid and the State Children's Health Insurance Program (CHIP) accounted for almost half of all spending on major low-income assistance programs.

Third, low-income aid became increasingly federalized. In the 1970s, the federal government assumed the costs of providing a cash income floor for the aged, blind, and disabled; by mid-decade the expanded food stamp program provided 100%-federally funded benefits nationwide using uniform benefit and eligibility rules; and housing aid shifted to 100%-federally financed vouchers.

In the last two decades (the 1990s and the 2000s), the major expansion of aid was done through refundable tax credits for families with children, 100% federally financed and administered through the tax code. The exception to the rule of increasing federalization—and it is a major exception—is that the costs of Medicaid and CHIP are shared with the states.

Fourth, for families with children, expansions of aid went to the working poor rather than the nonworking poor. The Medicaid expansions of the 1980s and early 1990s were for children who were not on cash assistance and thus targeted families with earnings. The Earned Income Tax Credit (EITC) and the refundable portion of the child credit require earnings to qualify for the credits. Food and housing assistance programs go to families with and without earned income, and increasingly to those who work.

Looking at CBO's budget projections of current policies, low-income aid would become increasingly dominated by health care. Medicaid, CHIP, and the new health care tax credit established in the 2010 health law would account for almost 7 out of 10 dollars spent on low-income aid by 2022.

Non-health programs would see their aggregate spending decline. This decline would result from three major factors: (1) declines in caseloads as the economy is expected to continue to recover from the 2007-2009 recession; (2) expiration of temporary benefit and funding increases in ARRA; and (3) the scheduled expiration in 2012 of the expansions of the child tax credit (and its refundable portion, the Additional Child Tax Credit, ACTC) and the EITC.

APPENDIX

The spending trends shown in this report are based on spending for 9 of the 10 largest (in terms of spending) programs providing low-income assistance catalogued in CRS Report R41625, *Federal Benefits and Services for People with Low Income: Programs, Policy, and Spending, FY2008-FY2009*, by Karen Spar. That report provides a "snapshot" of federal or federally assisted need-based programs with $100 million or more in obligations in FY2008 or FY2009. This report intends to complement the material in CRS Report R41625 by providing information on long-term spending trends.

The 10 largest need-tested programs discussed in CRS Report R41625 were (1) Medicaid; (2) SNAP; (3) SSI; (4) EITC; (5) Pell Grants; (6) the ACTC (the refundable portion of the child tax credit); (7) Title I-A Education for the Disadvantaged; (8) Medicare Part D, the Prescription Drug Low-Income Subsidy; (9) TANF; and (10) Section 8 Housing Choice Vouchers. CRS Report R41625 used federal obligations as its measure of spending for a program because they are the most consistent measure at the level of detail (program-level) used in that report. However, as mentioned in that report, obligations are difficult to track in a consistent manner over time.

The most consistent measure of federal spending available over time is outlays, which represent actual payments from the federal government, usually in the form of checks or electronic transfers of funds. Each year, the Office of Management and Budget (OMB) releases a database that shows historical outlays for each budget account for each fiscal year from FY1962 and later. Additionally, the Congressional Budget Office (CBO) makes its baseline budget projections in terms of outlays for each budget account.

The tradeoff here is that budget account outlays do not necessarily represent program-level activity. Some programs represent spending within only a part of an account. Moreover, the composition of accounts sometimes changes over time, which necessitates combining multiple accounts to provide consistent measures of spending over time.

Table A-1 shows the federal outlays for the selected major income assistance programs by budget account. It shows that three of the categories represent combinations of accounts.

Table A-1. Federal Outlays for Selected Major Low-Income Assistance Programs, By Budget Account, FY2011-FY2013 Dollars in millions

Program/Group	Treasury Identification for Budget Account	2011	CBO March 2012 Baseline	
			2012	2013
Medicaid/SCHIP				
Medicaid	75-0512-0-1-551	$274,964	$258,040	$276,064
Children's Health Insurance Fund[a]	75-0515-0-1-551	8,633	9,195	9,748
Total Medicaid/SCHIP		***283,597***	***267,235***	***285,812***
SNAP	12-3505-0-1-605	77,637	81,053	81,986
Student Financial Assistance	91-0200-0-1-502	37,894	37,421	38,146
Compensatory Education	91-0900-0-1-501	19,536	18,012	16,448
Assisted Housing[b]				
Tenant-Based Rental Assistance	86-0302-0-1-604	18,570	18,118	18,442
Project-based Rental Assistance	86-0303-0-1-604	8695	9,309	9,700
Housing Certificate Fund	86-0319-0-1-604	1,170	900	732
Housing for the Elderly	86-0320-0-1-604	934	850	783
Housing for Persons with Disabilities	86-0237-0-1-604	309	235	225
Revitalization of Severely Distressed	86-0218-0-1-604	177	155	135
Public Housing				
Green Retrofit Program for Multifamily	86-0306-0-1-604	147	32	0
Housing				
Public Housing Capital Fund	86-0304-0-1-604	4,176	2,650	2,200
Public Housing Operating Fund	86-0163-0-1-604	4,620	4,287	4,004
Native American Housing Block Grant	86-0313-0-1-604	854	645	618
Other Assisted Housing Programs	86-0206-0-1-604	496	460	417
Flexible Subsidy Fund	86-4044-0-3-604	-37	-30	-30
Total Assisted Housing		***40,111***	***37,611***	***37,226***
EITC	20-0906-0-1-609	55,652	55,686	58,243
Additional Child Tax Credit	20-0922-0-1-609	22,691	22,973	22,865

Table A-1. (Continued)

Program/Group	Treasury Identification for Budget Account	2011	CBO March 2012 Baseline	
			2012	2013
SSI	28-0406-0-1-609	56,462	50,407	57,162
Family Support[c]				
Family Support Account (Child Support Enforcement)	75-1501-0-1-609	4,182	4,226	4,277
TANF	75-1552-0-1-609	17,116	17,144	16,878
Contingency Fund	75-1522-0-1-609	1,956	1,134	786
CCDBG	75-1515-0-1-609	2,984	2,252	2,297
Child Care Entitlement to the States	75-1550-0-1-609	3,100	2,896	2,897
Federal Share of Child Support Collections	75-9992-8-1-609	-940	-867	-871
Total Family Support		***28,398***	***26,785***	***26,264***

Source: Congressional Research Service (CRS), based on data from the U.S. Office of Management and Budget (OMB) and the Congressional Budget Office (CBO).

[a.] Includes outlays for the children's health insurance contingency enrollment fund.

[b.] For prior years, includes outlays from the following accounts that no longer have spending associated with them: annual contribution to assisted housing, prevention of resident displacement, preserving housing investment, section 8 reserve preservation account, moving to work, rental housing assistance, and low-rent public housing loans and other expenses.

[c.] For prior years, includes outlays from the Job Opportunity and Basic Skills Training (JOBS) account.

Medicaid (the largest program) is combined in this report with the State Children's Health Insurance program (CHIP) because some CHIP programs are expansions of Medicaid. Housing assistance combines many accounts and represents far more spending than the Section 8 Housing Choice Vouchers discussed in CRS Report R41625. The account composition of housing aid has changed many times over the years, and a consistent measure of "housing assistance" requires combining both rent vouchers and support for families in public housing.

Finally, the "Family Support" account comprises more than TANF. In the federal budget, TANF's predecessor (Aid to Families with Dependent Children) was included in the same account as the Child Support Enforcement (CSE) program and child care for families receiving, transitioning from, or at-risk of receiving cash assistance. Therefore, the "Family Support" category covers TANF, CSE, and today's child care subsidy programs. TANF also consolidated funding in the pre-1996 program to provide employment services, education, and training for cash assistance recipients (the Job Opportunity and Basic Skills Training, or JOBS, program); funding for that program is included in the historical outlays of the "Family Support" category.

In addition, Pell Grants are the major component of the "Student Financial Assistance" account. Also included in the "Student Financial Assistance" account are federal supplemental educational opportunity grants (SEOGs) and college work study programs.

The largest component of the "Compensatory Education" (currently named "Accelerating Achievement and Ensuring Equity") account is the Title I-A grants to school districts with low-income children, but it also includes School Improvement Grants, Even Start, and the High School Graduation initiative, among other activities.

The Medicare Part D (prescription drug) low-income subsidy is not included in this report because it is not separately accounted for in the federal budget, but instead is subsumed in the much larger budget account that finances the Medicare prescription drug program. Unlike other programs, CRS Report R41625 did not use federal budget information to capture spending for this program. Rather, it used information from the annual report of the Medicare trustees.

End Notes

[1] The selection of programs for this report was based on the largest programs identified in CRS Report R41625, *Federal Benefits and Services for People with Low Income: Programs, Policy, and Spending, FY2008-FY2009*, by Karen Spar. See the **Appendix** to this report for a discussion of the selection of programs.

[2] The order of the programs listed here is the same order in which they appear on this report's graphic figures.

[3] The Patient Protection and Affordable Care Act (P.L. 111-148) as amended by the Heath Care and Education Reconciliation Act of 2010 (P.L. 111-152).

[4] See CRS Report R40942, *Private Health Insurance Provisions in the Patient Protection and Affordable Care Act (PPACA)*, by Hinda Chaikind and Bernadette Fernandez ...

[5] There are also rules that restrict noncitizen eligibility for other low-income benefit programs; see CRS ReportRL33809, *Noncitizen Eligibility for Federal Public Assistance: Policy Overview and Trends*, by Ruth Ellen Wasem.

[6] The trend in housing outlays shows the effects of a one-time payment made in FY1985, which resulted from a change in financing of public housing construction and modernization activities.

[7] For a discussion, see CRS Report R41873, *The Child Tax Credit: Current Law and Legislative History* , by Margot L. Crandall-Hollick.

[8] See CRS Report R42050, *Budget "Sequestration" and Selected Program Exemptions and Special Rules*, coordinated by Karen Spar.

INDEX

D

E

F

G

H